A LEADERSHIP VACl

Why American Management Keeps Trying to Suck Employees Out of the Equation

Chuck Ballard, PE

Characters depicted in this book are fictional, composites from observations made by the author over many years, companies and situations. Any resemblance to actual events or persons, living or dead, is coincidental to illustrating the author's points.

"A Leadership Vacuum," by Chuck Ballard, PE. ISBN 978-1-60264-422-9 (softcover); 978-1-60264-423-6 (ebook).

Published 2009 by Virtualbookworm.com Publishing Inc., P.O. Box 9949, College Station, TX 77842, US. ©2009, Chuck Ballard, PE. All rights reserved. No part of this publication may be reproduced, stored in a retrieval system, or transmitted in any form or by any means, electronic, mechanical, recording or otherwise, without the prior written permission of Chuck Ballard, PE.

Manufactured in the United States of America.

FOREWORD

Mushrooms?!!? Why mushrooms on the cover of a book dealing with the difference between leadership and managership? I would ask anyone who has been in an American company of any size for more than 1 year this question: How long were you there before you heard someone say something like "They treat us like mushrooms. They keep us in the dark, and they feed us plenty of male cow excrement"? That's why.

This book is the result of over 40 years of observations within Fortune 500 companies, and dealing with their vendors, consultants, employees, supervisors and managers. These observations have been done from both the inside and the outside of many of these large monoliths of American business, and, the admittedly deliberately changed, composite scenarios, used as object lessons here, illustrate the pervasive lack of basic leadership behaviors and skills shown today in American business and management in general. They do not represent any one firm or another – the problem is too pervasive for that to be the case.

Most American managers firmly believe they are leaders because they are managers. Many believe that leaders can be appointed. Others believe that all a leader needs is a vision, and the management skills to direct people how to achieve that vision.

A more pervasive problem is an unstated belief that 'leadership' is an archaic term incompatible with the collaborative teamwork ethos of the 21st century.

This book attempts to dispel those myths. Only you, the reader, will be able to judge that claim.

> *"Leadership is not managership. Leadership is the ability to get someone to do something they really don't want to do." Norman Schwartzkoph, Gen. US Army (retired) at the National School Boards Association Annual Meeting, Orlando FL*

ACKNOWLEDGMENTS

The author wishes to thank the many long-suffering friends, colleagues and enemies who have suffered with him in the vacuum. Without you, there would have been a lot fewer stories to relate.

PREFACE

It Doesn't Have to Be This Way, And It Will Get Worse if It Continues

The sub-title of this book is "Why American Management Keeps Trying to Suck Employees Out of The Equation". Why would I even make that assertion?

I contend that if you look at nearly every major change in business, from HR practices to work environments, over the past 40 years, you will find a high percentage of things that either deliberately, or inadvertently, try to minimize the impact of individual employees on the business, and to minimize managerial contact with employees to situations of planning, organization, staffing, direction or control. The emphasis is on managership, not leadership.

When employees used to be fired, their supervisor would walk them to their desk to clean out their belongings, now it is generally a security guard. When your supervisor used to assign you work, he called you in to his or her office,. Now you will get an email with a link from an automated work tracking system.

Managers used to be able to reward outstanding contributors for special talents. Now evaluation systems and salary ranges are geared toward keeping averages in line. "Market Evaluations" and "Hay Ranges" commoditize employees.

The net result of changes like this is to devalue leadership versus managership. I believe this is a mistake. I hope that you too will believe it is a mistake after reading this book.

> *"Hope is a state of mind, not of the world. Hope, in this deep and powerful sense, is not the same as joy that things are going well, or willingness to invest in enterprises that are obviously heading for success, but rather an ability to work for something because it is good." – Vaclav Havel*

"Lead and inspire people. Don't try to manage and manipulate people. Inventories can be managed but people must be lead." – Ross Perot

CHAPTER 1

A Break In The Action At Ponderous Power and Light

Ponderous Power and Light is a Fortune 500 company. In the era of deregulation, it is a well-managed company that regularly pays dividends to its shareholders, has well-paid executives who make multi-million dollar salaries, and generously rewards the members of its board of directors. In almost every Wall Street measure you can think of, it is a successful company. But there is something wrong that isn't obvious, and we are going to start the journey to see what that is, with a conversation taking place during a lunch break at an all day meeting of the top executives of Ponderous' Nuclear Division.

At this meeting, Bob Bigman, the senior VP of the Nuclear Division, has gathered his direct reports to work together to set goals for the next fiscal year. Bob is a long-term employee of Ponderous, having worked in the non-nuclear part of the company before transferring over to the Nuclear Division when its plants started construction. He worked himself up from the start-up organization to plant superintendent, then VP of Operations, and now is the Chief Nuclear Officer (CNO).

Johnny Walker, the VP of Engineering, is a relative newcomer to Ponderous. He was hired away from a southern utility to bring some 'fresh perspective' to the Nuclear Department. He likes to portray himself as a simple 'country boy' in public meetings, but anyone who has ever gotten on his bad side knows that the persona is just an act.

Hank Munster, the current VP of operations, was Bigman's assistant plant superintendent when Bigman was running the plant, and he has been riding on Bigman's coat-tails for years. In a meeting, if you watch him, you will see that he is observing his mentor to decide which way he should go on important issues.

Rounding out the group at the main table is Randal James, the Manager of Regulatory Issues. He's been with Ponderous about 10 years, and is known for his ability to finesse license changes through the bureaucracy of the Nuclear Regulatory Commission, and even more widely throughout the company for his ability to avoid blame for bad news with upper management.

Before lunch, James had delivered a report on an employee attitude survey that had been run by an outside consulting firm. That report had indicated that there were several basic morale issues for employees across the department. Delivery of lunch had interrupted discussion of these results. Several other lower level staff people had joined the group for lunch because they were scheduled to present items that had been delayed by the slow progress of the meeting. As lunch ended, this is what the staff members overheard:

> Bigman: "That was a nice spread for lunch Randall. Thank your secretary for arranging to have it delivered here so we could maximize our meeting time."

> James: "Thanks Bob. Jeanne is very efficient at getting these things done. Did you have a good weekend?"

> Bigman: "Yes I did. Went out to see that new Civil War movie, Gettysburg. Really a great movie. The battle scenes were very realistic. It really showed you it was touch and go for the Union to win that battle."

> Walker: "y'all know that if they'd had a few more of our Tennessee Volunteer sharp-shooters in Pickett's brigade, the Yankees would have lost that fight."

Munster: "I agree with you Bob, it was a great movie. That charge the Rebels made across that field was just about the bravest thing I've ever seen."

Walker: "Pickett's Charge, that's what it was called."

Bigman: "You know, I wonder what it would take, I mean for our people, to have the same level of devotion to their jobs, as those men in Picket's Charge had that day?"

<Storyline note: A silent mental scream echoes through the minds of just about all the staff members there – PICKETT!!>

James: "Yeah, something like that would take care of this morale finding"

Munster: "I'm sure that new video tape you've made Bob, explaining the new goal structure, and how it will improve performance, will do a lot to help."

Walker: "Sometimes, with a stubborn horse, or a mule, you've got to use tighter reins to get the critter to do what you want him to."

<Storyline note: At this point, the conversation breaks down discussing whether Johnny would be wearing overalls to the next meeting. We will come back to this meeting in a bit, but let's discuss what is missing here>

What was it that staff members could immediately see and relate to, but high level managers could not?

Leadership. Each of these top-level managers heard the name, Pickett, but did not associate it with the leader, George Pickett, who was not on that cornfield when the men of his brigade made their charge into the massed firepower of the Union position. It was Pickett that convinced his men to make the attempt, as William Faulkner said:

> *"For every Southern boy fourteen years old, not once but whenever he wants it, there is the instant when it's still not yet two o'clock on that July afternoon in 1863, the brigades are in position behind the rail fence, the guns are laid and ready in the woods and the furled flags are already loosened to break out and Pickett himself with his long oiled ringlets and his hat in one hand probably and his sword in the other looking up the hill waiting for Longstreet to give the word and it's all in the balance, it hasn't happened yet, it hasn't even begun yet, it not only hasn't begun yet but there is still time for it not to begin against that position and those circumstances which made more men than Garnett and Kemper and Armistead and Wilcox look grave yet it's going to begin, we all know that, we have come too far with too much at stake and that moment doesn't need even a fourteen-year-old boy to think this time." –*
> *Intruder in the Dust*

The basic problem is that these managers think that they are leaders. They have vision, they can issue clear orders, they know how to make good presentations, they have all their facts organized, and most of all, they have been successful doing things the way that they currently do them. That makes them leaders in their minds. They often even call themselves the "Leadership Team".

The top-down, control structure of American business encourages this fallacy. Terms like 'captain of industry' or 'leadership team' continuously appear in articles, pronouncements and messages to reinforce the idea that leadership is a control function, primarily.

The problem with leadership as merely a control function is that it is confusing the result with the method. As Dwight Eisenhower said, in a news conference:

> *"Mr. Brandt, leadership is a word and a concept that has been more argued than almost any other I know. I am not one of the desk-pounding type that likes to stick out his jaw and look like he is bossing the show. I would far rather get behind and, recognizing the frailties and the requirements of human nature, I would rather try to persuade a man to go along, because once I have persuaded him he will stick. If I **scare** him, he will stay just as long as he is **scared**, and then he is gone." – The*

President's News Conference of November 14, 1956

The key concept that differentiates leadership from control, or managership, is embodied in the words used by Eisenhower and Schwartzkoph over 40 years apart. Both men were acknowledged leaders, who formed coalitions of men with widely differing personalities and beliefs, that successfully prosecuted difficult wars. Those words were "persuade" and "convince".

Leaders do not work by simply 'ordering' people to do things. Leaders persuade people to do what they want, or convince them to follow their orders. The difference between these two approaches, leadership and managership, is profound, and so is the depth of misunderstanding of the difference in the average American manager.

Back in the 1980s, I took a college course titled "Supervision". The text we used categorized the duties of a supervisor or manager as: Planning, Organization, Staffing, Direction and Control. When asked to describe leadership, the vast majority of American managers will often use terms, like "Vision", "Clear Direction" or "Master

Strategist" to describe their idea of what qualities a leader has. What this amounts to is categorizing leadership as basically just outstanding managership.

How did we get so far off track that we no longer recognize, at least intellectually, what leadership is?

Let's begin our trek to understanding back at that management meeting at Ponderous Power and Light.

> *"A great leader never sets himself above his followers*
> *except in carrying responsibilities."*
> — *Jules Ormont*

"Leadership is a privilege, not a right"
— *Sergio Marchionne-Fiat*

CHAPTER 2

Leaders are Out in FRONT of the Troops

As we left our group of senior Ponderous managers, they had dissected the Civil War battle of Gettysburg. They had moved on to Sherman's March to the Sea, through Georgia:

> *Walker: "You know, you Yankees might have won the War Between the States, but we got the last laugh. A whole lot of your military industrial complex sits in the South and pumps billions of federal dollars into our economies.*
>
> *Bigman: "(laughing) Yeah, you're probably right on that one. You Rebs always were tricky. I remember that huge army base near Columbus, what was its' name?"*
>
> *Walker: "Fort Benning"*
>
> *Bigman: "That's it. I had a tour of that base one time that a friend of mine who was retired Army gave me. There was this big statue in front of one of the buildings there. He said it's real name was 'The Infantryman' but everyone at the base called it 'Follow Me'. I never did understand why they would call a statue of a soldier 'Follow Me'. You have any idea?"*

11

Walker: "No. Good soldiers follow orders. Must be an Army joke"

Bigman: "Right. Let's get back to the agenda."

Fort Benning is the home of the Army Infantry School, where Army officers get their first training in leadership skills. In front of Building 4 is a monument celebrating the courage and leadership of the citizen soldiers of America. It is a large statue of an infantryman leading others into battle. The arm is uplifted in a 'come with me' gesture and the head is turned back to look back at the troops he is urging into battle. It renders the spirit of the infantry leader in combat, leading from in front of his troops.

What did our Captains of Industry miss this time?

In order to be a leader, you have to have followers. Leaders cannot be appointed by other leaders. Leaders have to be elected by a group of followers. The followers follow their leader. They are not directed to follow, they are convinced to follow.

The cult of managership in American business today has buried this distinction to the point where almost no one thinks twice when they hear that someone has been

<u>appointed</u> to 'the leadership team'. Leadership is just another buzzword for being the boss. Managers are selected or appointed all the time. It's the same thing, right?

Leaders have to have qualities that create followers. Leaders have to have skills that harness their qualities to convince people to follow them. Developing these qualities and skills generally takes a lot of hard work. "Natural" leaders are probably as rare as "common sense" often seems to be. Most real-world leaders have had goals that stimulated them to exercise increasing levels of leadership because they needed others to help them achieve those goals.

One of the most common fallacies held by managers, is that leadership skills, if they even think in those terms, are some form of talent, 'soft' skill, or mainly some form of personal charisma, not a mental discipline. Managers whose goal is primarily upward mobility in an organization or society, often denigrate real leadership, particularly when shown by subordinates, and tend to only respect those who show partiality to heavy control strategies. I can't begin to count the number of times I have heard a variation of the theme that someone was looking for someone to "kick ass and take names" in the organizations I have worked with.

History is replete with counter examples to these managerial misconceptions. Joan of Arc couldn't have kicked the butt of anyone in the army she raised to restore the French monarchy. Ghengis Khan was not very soft. George Patton did not have a lot of people skills. Yet each of these acknowledged leaders found ways to convince people to follow them.

For a core group of followers, at least, a leader has to deal with people as individuals. This is something that is harder to do than trying to treat everyone as though they were the same. It can take a lot of work, particularly if you are not skilled in differentiating people and how to deal with those differences.

Inherent laziness and lack of understanding, again of the differences between leadership and managership have led to the American business phenomenon that I call the Replacement Employee Unit (REU) Theory of Management. This is an offshoot of the "No One is Irreplaceable" school which holds that one employee cannot be valuable enough to be given special consideration for their talents or their skills significantly above another employee.

The theory apparently goes that one REU is just as good as any other REU, and that you can move any REU into any position for your managership convenience, at will.

As evidence of the penetration of this theory in American business, I would point to the salary compression schemes practiced by quite a number of the Fortune 500. These are usually characterized by 'position ranking', 'salary ranges' and 'midpoints'. These schemas are not in and of themselves sufficient, however. What generally accompanies them are rigid criteria for individual salary maximum changes, lower than inflationary percentage additions to the salary pool to be distributed, and 'performance review' processes that are basically meaningless and decoupled from the actual salary performance. What generally accompanies this process is statistical compression to the 'midpoints' and mediocrity.

All this, to avoid having to do the extra effort, to recognize people as individuals. Or, at least, for all but a few 'individuals' at the top of the managerial pyramid, but more on that later.

Yes, it is dangerous to have any business or process totally dependent on just one person. That's why you should have good succession plans throughout your entire organization, not just for top managers, and good workforce development and training programs. Assuming, on the other hand, that you can replace anyone in the organization without significant extra cost, is just not usually true. This belief is all too common, though.

One current example of this is the number of companies who are having to bring back retired employees, generally at a premium, in order to deal with work situations that the people who replaced them cannot handle. Whether from a lack of skill, knowledge or experience, the replacement unit isn't able to fully deliver.

This failure isn't generally the fault of the employees. It is the fault of managers. It is a fault of leadership to not have some fundamental understanding of what is involved in doing the work your subordinates must do, and what kind of people it takes to do the work.

The mistake most managers, as opposed to leaders, make, is the fallacy that to have this understanding, it requires that they, the managers, have done the same type of work themselves at one time. This is not true. What you need to know is who <u>on your team</u> knows that.

In fact, most of the blunders I have seen managers make in this regard are because they think they are still experts in a very technical field that they once maintained expertise in, and don't listen to their team.

I guarantee to you that after 6 months of being promoted away from any process area, you are no longer as expert in that area as you still think you are.

The most egregious example of this that I ever witnessed was as a vendor technical representative working in a field assignment. A highly-capable team of the customer's engineers had reviewed a proposal for a new digital feedwater control system for a powerplant. They had facts and figures that showed that by upgrading the control system at the plant, fewer plant outages and power swings would occur, and the control system would pay for itself in just 2-3 years of better operation. After presenting this material, they came to the bottom line, the cost, 50 thousand dollars.

At that point, the VP of Operations declared, "I'm an old I&C (instrumentation and control) engineer, and no <expletive-deleted> control system for a simple turbine should cost $50 thousand." End of meeting.

Now this gentleman had not touched a control system design in the past 15 years, having moved up into the ranks of management and steadily progressed to his current position. There was no way that he could have done the jobs he held in between and have kept current with all the developments in control system design. He was no longer the expert he thought he was.

Note that he did not use his expertise and experience to review and question the <u>methodology</u> that was used by his team, or to develop probing questions to determine if they had done their homework. He just substituted his 'expertise' for theirs because he could.

He didn't value his team as 'experts'. They were just another group of replaceable employee units. No flaw in the team's logic had been observed. No fact had been proven false. This VP had just reduced the value of a group of employees to essentially nothing. Just imagine how inspiring it would be to be told, as an employee unit, that you had another chance to make a technical presentation to this manager.

A manager can assess and rank the assets he or she is given in terms of employees. A leader values the intrinsic worth of each of his followers, and works to obtain the maximum value from that worth for his cause.

Therein lies the reason why leaders can accomplish more than managers. By simply ranking their personnel, and often discounting the lower-ranked individuals, managers tend to waste potential, particularly if their ranking is influenced by personal dislike. Leaders seek to motivate all of their personnel to provide their best efforts to the cause.

Leaders are aware that they can be powerful sources of demotivation also. Managers are not often as aware of the constant scrutiny of their subordinates for information and inspiration, as we will see as we move on to the Executive Floor of Ponderous.

However, a clear distinction between management and leadership may nevertheless prove useful. This would allow for a reciprocal relationship between leadership and manage-ment, implying that an effective manager should possess leadership skills, and an effective leader should demonstrate management skills. One clear distinction could provide the following definition: Management involves power by position.

Leadership involves power by influence.

Abraham Zaleznik (Zaleznik, A. [1977] "Managers and Leaders: Is there a difference?", Harvard Business Review, May-June, 1977)

I BEEN WORKING IN THIS FACTORY/ PRETTY
CLOSE TO 15 YEARS
IVE SOME OF MY BEST FRIENDS WOMEN/
STANDING IN A POOL OF TEARS
IVE SEEN A LOT OF KINFOLKS DYING/ I HAD A
LOT OF BILLS TO PAY
LORD, I'D GIVE THE SHIRT RIGHT OFFIN MY
BACK/ IF I HAD THE NERVE TO SAY:
TAKE THIS JOB AND SHOVE IT
– David Allen Coe Lyrics Song by Johnny Paycheck

CHAPTER 3

The Rules Are Different For Me

It is ten o'clock on Thursday morning, and Harry Medici, the Manager of Buildings and Maintenance for Ponderous, has been called up to the executive level of the Ponderous headquarters building by the CEO, Bob Baker.

Ponderous has had a couple of good years, and is embarking on a long-overdue renovation of its office facilities. Aware of the positive public relations associated with businesses conserving energy and resources, Ponderous has committed to performing 'green' renovations where ever possible. It is now time for the renovations to take place on the executive level, and Baker has asked Medici, the overall project manager for the renovations, to stop by his office to 'discuss a few details'.

21

Baker: (To Medici standing outside his office) "Harry, come on in. Good to see you. We're still on schedule to start work on this floor in two weeks?"

Medici: "We're ready to go as soon as we can move your furniture to hotel space on the second floor. We've got all the material on hand, and our construction crews and contractors are just finishing up the punch list on the 12th and 14th floors. If we had a 13th floor, that would be done too."

Baker: "Just like a hotel too. We don't want any superstitious employees spooked by a bad floor number, do we? (laughing) But calling the second floor hotel space is a little too generous. Johnny Walker over in Nuclear would call that putting lipstick on a pig! (laughing again)"

Medici: "Come on Bob, it's the best we can do. We have to vacate the entire floor while we rip out the old plumbing. Some of that pipe is older than the pyramids, and it has asbestos insulation..."

Baker: (interrupting) "OK, OK, Harry, I know. But it's the plumbing, or really part of it, that I wanted to talk to you about. What kind of fixtures are you planning to put in on this floor?"

Medici: "Why, the same thing we've been putting in on all the other floors, and all the new buildings in the company. Low-flow toilets with infrared automatic flush controls, low-flow sinks with infrared controlled valves, waterless urinals and...."

Baker: (interrupting again) "Yeah, those waterless urinals. Do I have to have them on my floor?"

Medici: "Well, those are what we specified for all the floors. They save hundreds, maybe as much as a thousand gallons of water a year. Each."

Baker: "Well, I've had to use them on some of the remodeled floors and I don't like them. If they aren't regularly serviced, they stink to high heaven, and I like the feeling of hitting that lever and flushing it away. I DON'T have to have them on this floor, do I?"

Medici: "uh, well Bob, uh, if you don't want them, I guess we can order some standard units for this floor...."

Baker: "With manual valves, right?"

Medici: "uh, yes Bob, of course."

Baker: "Great Harry! I knew I could count on you to do the right thing. Hey let Helen know on the way out what tee time you want for the Operation Assist golf tournament next week. We want 100% participation by the leadership team. Gotta show that Ponderous is a good corporate citizen you know"

Medici: "Right Bob. See you on the course" (exits)

Like in the old industrial safety quizzes, How Many Things Can You Find Wrong In This Picture?

For starters, if you were Harry Medici, would you now be convinced beyond a shadow of a doubt that there were different rules for those at the top of the company versus everyone else? Do you think that you might let that color your attitude just a tiny bit?

Which way might that lead you to act? Might resentment, hidden or otherwise, cause you to maliciously comply with some future directive that you knew from your training and experience was a bad move for the company? Or would you accept the situation as another case of Rank Hath Its Privilege (RHIP) and let that color your attitude as you deal with your direct subordinates and others of lower rank within the company?

Would either of these responses be good for Ponderous as a company?

A leader would understand that people do watch and modify their behavior because of what a positional role model does and how he or she acts. Managers may know this also, but they don't intrinsically understand that the change is done in accordance with the <u>watcher's</u> perception of the behavior, not the model's perception of his or her, own behavior.

Then, there is the idea that standards, rules or policies are not to be uniformly applied across the company. That somehow persons in places of power are exempt from having to follow practices that they have often enforced on the rest of the company, often for the purpose of enhancing their public reputation, or that of 'their' company.

The idea inherent in the phrase "Do as I say, not do as I do", has been motivator for scatological remarks about hypocrisy since just about the first time mankind started writing down commentary on leaders (generals) and managers (overseers).

The persistent theme of many Greek tragedies, "hubris", the overweening pride that led otherwise great men to downfall, usually occurred when the protagonist became convinced he was good enough or great enough to go against the gods (the rules).

Why, if philosophers, moralists and playwrights, have warned against this pitfall for centuries, does it still continue to plague us?

I contend that it can be explained in the different world views of a manager versus a leader.

Lord Acton, writing to Bishop Creighton in 1887, coined the maxim "Power tends to corrupt, and absolute power corrupts absolutely".

Managers tend to view power as related to position, and achievement of position, to have been accomplished solely on the basis of their own individual efforts.

I once had a very revealing private conversation with a high-priced 'management consultant' who had been brought in to a company I worked for by one of its vice presidents. The ostensible goal of the 'engagement' was to offer advice to the VP and his direct reports as to how they could improve their 'leadership and management' skills. After several weeks of observation of this management 'team', I could tell that the consultant was very frustrated.

I asked if he was having any difficulty getting any changes to occur. He looked at me for a time and then said: "These people have spent their careers getting to where they are by doing what they are doing now. How difficult do you think it is to convince them that they need to change what they are doing?" I knew it would be extremely difficult. In a couple of weeks, the consultant's services were no longer required.

Leaders know that their leadership positions have been achieved by convincing their followers, and that the efforts the leaders have coaxed from their followers have led to the leader's success. Leaders, knowing that they have to keep their followers convinced, are much less likely to think that they can flaunt their own rules in front of those below them, or keep their rule-breaking a secret.

Even if the executive washroom is locked, someone has to go in and clean it, and it likely isn't the CEO of the company. Someone has to repair the leaky faucets, and it usually isn't the President. Trust me, people will find out, and word will spread, along with a growing disrespect for ALL of the rules, regulations and standards of the company.

What is really called for is an epiphany, in the truly classical definition of that term. What that really means for American business, we will have to discuss later, as we still have miles to go in this discussion.

"If you focus on principles, you empower everyone who understands those principles to act without constant monitoring, evaluating, correcting, or controlling" – *Stephen R. Covey*

The Rules and Justice Should Be For Everyone

Poetic Justice, with her lifted scale,
Where in nice balance, truth with gold she weighs.
And solid pudding against empty praise
–The Dunciad, by Alexander Pope

"You don't lead by hitting people over the head - that's assault, not leadership."
–Dwight D. Eisenhower

CHAPTER 4

Why Can We Only Put Smiles On The Faces of People Who Are Leaving?

It has to be there. Somewhere. It has to be buried in some training material, some self-help management book, some company policy, some memo from HR, somewhere. It has to be something managers are taught, practically from birth. Otherwise, why would the condition be so prevalent in American business today?

If you're a Ponderous employee, taking a brief walk on the mall during lunch, and you see another Ponderous employee coming toward you wearing a "shit-eating grin", you know immediately what the cause is. The other employee is leaving the company. It may be for retirement, it may be for another job, but you know that they are leaving.

In the course of my career, I put the title question of this chapter to 3 different VP-level managers. Not one of those successful, highly-compensated, high-level people had the slightest idea of how to respond to the question. Not one of them even attempted to answer it.

Part of the reason that this is such a difficult question for managers to deal with, is that 'deep down', the vast majority of managers do not believe that they have any responsibility for the 'morale' of the organization. This actually is another of those core belief differences that distinguish a manager from a leader.

A manager provides clear direction on what an employee is supposed to do. How is it his or her problem that the employee is unhappy about doing it? It's not their job to make the employee happy, is it?

No, it really isn't, at least as far as the version of the definition of 'happy' that most managers try to turn to in order to explain their lack of responsibility for the condition. That is the 'marked by joy or pleasure' type of 'happy'.

But what about the 'eagerly disposed to act or to be of service' acceptable definition for 'happy'? Doesn't that just sound more productive when it could be used to describe an employee? Isn't productivity a management responsibility anymore?

If anyone tries to tell you that employee morale doesn't have a major affect on productivity, in just about every setting imaginable, please ask them what they are smoking. I want the franchise for my state.

The problem for managers is that you really can't affect morale through planning, organizing, staffing, directing or controlling. In short, you can't manage your way out of morale problems.

Let's see what happens at Ponderous, when the managers decide to tackle their morale problem. An outside survey company has returned results of a survey of employees in the Engineering Department, and the Manager of Engineering, Sam Polowski, has called an all-employee meeting to respond to the situation:

> *Polowski: "...so as you can see, overall employee satisfaction with management in Engineering has declined for the third year in a row. Your leadership team has been discussing these results for several weeks now, and we have come up with the answer **to** the morale problem.*

We all know that if people are motivated to do something, they do it. So, we have developed the Ponderous Improvement Strategy Subsidy program. Next year...if the employee satisfaction rating with management improves by 10% on the survey, your salary bonus will go up by 2%."

Voice from the back of the auditorium: "So, if I rate management 10% higher, my salary goes up?"

Polowski: "That's right."

Voice: "OK, give me the survey right now. I know how to fill it out."

See, if you incentivize employees, they know what to do. Rate management higher. You can control that response with incentives, right?

Managers love responses that they can control. So when they look through that lens at morale, they think morale is a response that they ought to be able to control. A leader would view the situation as a response that needs to be created by convincing people that things are actually improving.

Trying to 'control' morale is generally self-defeating. The more control applied, the more morale deteriorates, even more control is applied, and so on, in a destructive spiral.

A sad corollary to this death spiral is that some evidence of high morale, like spontaneous outbursts of silly behavior (like filling a co-worker's cubicle with balloons while they are on vacation), is a sign to some managers that the 'situation is out of control', a fate worse than death, apparently.

American business has embraced control to practically the exclusion of all other considerations. That is a serious mistake in terms of long-term productivity potential for any organization.

Consideration of leadership approaches to morale would have to include approaches to inspire enthusiasm in the organization. Yet, how many times have you seen management positions filled by people who 'know how to kick ass and take names' instead of lead? Control for control's sake is not leadership.

In a Dilbert™ cartoon (6-23-05), Dogbert™, as an executive search consultant, says "You want someone with a reputation for toughness, who knows how to get the most out of people". The next panel shows Dogbert holding a torch in a Transylvanian castle, while the vampire holding his next victim says "Come back later, I'm still getting the most out of this one."

(The reason that Scott Adams, the creator of Dilbert, is not likely to suffer the burnout that afflicted other cartoonists, like Gary Larsen {The Far Side™}, is that he literally gets dozens of new humorous examples of management fumbles with leadership issues, sent to him every day in emails from your employees. A literary gold mine provided gratis by American managers. Can't blame the Chinese for this one.)

Leadership, by its very existence in an organization, improves morale. So why wouldn't a company want to develop leadership skills in its employees? Why can't some companies keep employees that show leadership ability? We will explore that in the next couple of chapters.

> *"The day soldiers stop bringing you their problems is the day you have stopped leading them. They have either lost confidence that you can help them or concluded that you do not care. Either case is a failure of leadership."*
> *– General Colin Powell – A Leadership Primer*

"The leader is fairest, but all are divine."
– Matthew Arnold

INTERLUDE I

Goodbye Cruel World

Ponderous is certainly not the company your father or grandfather might have joined coming out of World War II. 'Utilities' as they were called then, were very stable, comfortable, laid back work environments for the most part. You went to work for them, did your job (mostly), didn't screw anything up badly or take bribes, worked there 35 or 40 years and got a pension. The company was guaranteed a decent rate of return on its investment by the Public Utility Commission. Investors, including many little old ladies, held your stock as a 'safe' investment, yielding steady dividends, without much price volatility.

Deregulation has changed all that. Ponderous is now a 'holding company' and bills itself as "Energy Purveyors to the World". All of the 'generation assets', i.e. the plants that actually make electricity with generators, are in a separate, unregulated subsidiary company. The regulated part of the business, the "meters and wires" part of the company, is still regulated, but it too is a separate company and represents less than 10% of the total Ponderous revenue stream.

When this all happened in the 1990s, a lot of changes occurred within and without of the company. First of all, the stock became a lot more volatile. Like many companies in those heady days going into the start of the 3rd millennium (AD), the concept of dividends became passé. Real, knowledgeable investors held stock for appreciation. Wall Street analysts understood this, but the little old ladies only found out about it when their dividend checks started getting smaller. Ponderous applied its new 'found' cash, those dividends they weren't paying, as a good source of money to 'invest' in new businesses, including buying shares in third-world utility companies.

Inside Ponderous, a number of higher management personnel were not comfortable with these changes. Those who didn't 'go with the flow' were replaced, shunted aside, or 'left to pursue other opportunities'. New people were brought in from outside to bring a 'fresh outlook' on operating Ponderous in a competitive environment. Some new approaches were definitely needed, but these new managers also brought with them entirely new attitudes about what the true value of employees was.

To be fair, some of the old Ponderous managers hadn't valued employees too much either, but the paternalistic culture had included values that blocked most unfair treatment, and kept all but the most restless employees content. During the 'old' days, college advisors used to tell students that utilities normally hired from the bottom third of the class, because 'those were the only people that would stick with them'. You see, loyalty was valued by both sides.

The new managers brought with them the concept of "human capital", a term designed to remove the actual humanity part of the equation, and treat employees as another piece of equipment. Loyalty and respect were foreign terms in this context. No one expects a lathe to be loyal or to respect anyone.

So, the new managers, and the old managers who didn't think much of individual employees, began to change the culture at Ponderous. Very soon, the entire situation began to deteriorate, at least from the employee point of view. Years of faithful service didn't mean anything anymore.

"What have you done for me in the last micro-second" appeared to be the mantra.

These developments coalesced with trends in society toward absolute risk-aversion and over-emphasis by the media on how dangerous human beings can be. "Going Postal" had entered the lexicon, and now the first concern was how much of a security risk was each employee.

The net result was that loyalty was no longer valued, and the quantity of loyalty that had been built up over the years was not-so-slowly erased. But the funny thing was, managers acted as if their employees should be loyal to the company. Some were actually shocked that employees on expense accounts would start charging expensive meals at out of town restaurants after one of their expense accounts had been rejected for not obtaining a receipt from a Kentucky Fried Chicken ™ location while 'trying to save the company money'.

Where this really came into sharp focus was when Ponderous started to have financial difficulties. The stock market was down, the dividend was flat, and Ponderous stock was falling so much that some executives stock bonuses were already under water. Something had to be done!

Ponderous officers decided that layoffs were necessary. Not wanting to take direct moral responsibility for cutting people themselves, nor apparently believing that they had any such responsibility, the way to accomplish the goal was to send down the line budget cut 'targets' that would be impossible to meet without reductions in personnel.

So, in an organization that had rarely, if ever, let anyone go, quite a number of people were going to be exiting quite soon.

A leader might ask what could be done with the employees to avoid layoffs. Perhaps people could be asked to volunteer to be laid off. Perhaps employees would agree to a percentage pay cut to preserve jobs for everyone. Maybe employees have suggestions that would save enough money to avoid layoffs. None of those things were tried at Ponderous.

What did happen is that starting on the last week of the month, employees in various departments were called in, at specified times, like 9 a.m., 11 a.m. and 1 p.m. of a given day, to a conference room or a private office, for an unannounced meeting with the department supervisor. Generally present was the employee's direct supervisor, as a witness for the company. The employee, of course, had no witness for himself.

Reading from a 'canned' script, the employee was told by the department supervisor that his or her services were no longer required by Ponderous. In most cases the 'witness', the employee's direct supervisor, remained totally silent during this meeting.

The employee was told to surrender his or her badge, keys, corporate credit card and cell phone. Their supervisor was to escort them to their desk, sometimes with security personnel in attendance, and make sure that the employee surrendered the company equipment and logged off any computer system without performing any other functions. In many cases, computer security access was actually cancelled before the employee got to the meeting room.

In some cases, employees were given time to retrieve personal effects immediately, and in some cases they were not. The employees from any given 'time slot' were then escorted out of the company building and told to attend a meeting across the street at a local hotel that morning or afternoon, with HR representatives who would give them information about their separation benefits.

The main purpose of the meetings in the hotel was for HR to emphasize that the vast bulk of the separation benefits were contingent on the laid-off employees signing a 'separation agreement' absolving Ponderous of any possible liability for being sued by the employees. Extra pressure was put on by the corporate policy that ended all benefits, including medical 'as of the end of the month of termination', i.e., a few days away, except possibly for a brief extension of 4 weeks without the separation agreement. Oh, the employees did have 45 days in which to sign the separation agreement…

At least one poor soul even got laid off by telephone, while on medical leave. He got a call from a conference room at 9:30 a.m., with the same scripted presentation. He was even asked to come in to the hotel 'if possible' for the meeting with HR at 11:30, to 'get your binder'! There was a significant pause in the script presentation when the employee noted that he would have to contact his doctor to see if he was permitted to drive yet. Nothing changed in the script presentation, but 30 minutes later he got another call from the department supervisor that he should not come to the meeting and that a 'personal meeting with an HR representative' would be arranged for him next week when he was supposed to be cleared to 'come back to work' (sic).

Note all the common themes in these scenarios:

- The events were all timed and coordinated like a military strike. Nothing was to be allowed to interfere with the timing

- All employees were to be treated as potential security risks for sabotage or worse.

- Not even being out on sick leave well prior to the date intended for the layoff would be allowed to interfere with the timing of the notice.

- It didn't matter whether you were a short-time or long-time employee, you would be treated the same way. People with 25-35 years of committed service to the company went out the door this way.

- No explanations, regrets or apologies were offered for why the employees being laid off were being treated the way they were

The way Ponderous handled its layoffs is becoming all too typical in American business. Managers like those at

Ponderous do not appear to even consider basic human concerns that nearly any leader would start with from first principles.

Maneuvers like this have what is known in the military as a 'probability of kill of 2.0 (you and the enemy)', because both the employees being laid off and their fellow employees that remain are damaged by such tactics.

How would you feel if you saw your fellow employee treated like this, and you realize that is exactly how you are going to be treated, and how much this tells you about how much you are valued as an individual in today's corporations? No wonder that a recent employee loyalty survey conducted by the Loyalty Institute in Ann Arbor, Michigan, and sponsored by AON Consulting, found that employers that reduce their workforces can expect a sharp drop in commitment from the employees that remain!

"Make sure that they have somebody double-check their recommendations on who needs to go…" "Because I think what you're going to find here is that discrimination is not going to be coming down from the top, but I think it's going to be the petty tyrant who now has life-and-death power over his employees." - Bill Amlong

"Seagull Managers fly in, make a lot of noise, dump on everyone, then fly out."
– Ken Blanchard

"I would rather try to persuade a man to go along, because once I have persuaded him he will stick. If I scare him, he will stay just as long as he is scared, and then he is gone."
- President Dwight D. Eisenhower

CHAPTER 5

...I Am In Control Here...

"...in the White House..." That simple phrase, those last 5 words of which just about every reporter conveniently missed, went on to haunt retired General Alexander Haig after the assassination attempt on President Ronald Reagan. The whole statement was seen by some as an attempt by Haig, as Secretary of State, to exceed his Constitutional authority.

Haig was seeing it in another light:

> *"I wasn't talking about transition. I was talking about the executive branch, who is running the government. That was the question asked. It was not, 'Who' is in line should the President die?"*
> *–Alexander Haig, Alexander Haig interview with 60 Minutes April 23, 2001*

Who was in control? Control is a function of management. A major problem in American business is that control is being seen as the PRIMARY function of management.

What is even worse, the word control is becoming synonymous with coercion.

Coercion does have a time-honored spot in human history. In the early part of the Agrarian era, when man first learned to farm, power structures became more significant and more formalized. This probably occurred because life became more complex with larger numbers of people inhabiting the land in larger groupings, like villages and eventually cities.

In his course "Big History: The Big Bang, Life on Earth and the Rise of Humanity" (The Teaching Company, www.teach12.com), Professor David Christian identifies two distinct ways of mobilizing power that occurred identifiably in the Agrarian era:

A.   "Power from below" is power conceded more or less willingly by individuals or groups who expect to benefit from subordination to skillful leaders. People expect something in return for subordination, so power from below is a 'mutualistic' form of symbiosis. As societies become larger and denser, leadership became more important in order to achieve group goals, such as the building of irrigation systems or defense in war…

B.   "Power from above" depends on the capacity to make credible threats of coercion. That depends on the existence of disciplined groups of coercers, loyal to the leader and able to enforce the leader's will by force when necessary. In such an environment, people obey because they will be punished if they do not. This aspect of power highlights the coercive (or 'parasitic') element in power relationships...

C.   Building coercive groups is complex and costly, and the earliest forms of power emerged before such groups existed. That is why the first power elites depended mainly on power from below."

People who can naturally lead are rarer than those who by nature can plan and organize. As human society became more complex, more and more planning and organizing was necessary. This is when we started to get more managers than leaders in everyday affairs and business.

The real problems started when the managers started to try to acquire more personal power, and without marked leadership skills to create large groups of followers, their only reliable option was "Plan B". (That is also the reason, I believe, that ever since written records have been created, there have been complaints recorded about bureaucrats.)

So, how does control get 'out of control' in modern American business? Let's go into a manager's office in the Engineering Division of Ponderous. Don Redwing is the manager of Control Systems Engineering. Joe Tosbar is one of Don's senior engineer's. Joe is requesting Don's approval on a work package that Joe has just completed. The work package was initiated by an Engineering Work Order (EWO) that Don delegated to Joe a couple of weeks ago:

Joe: "Dan, have you had a chance to review the resolution of EWO 7734? I left it in your inbox a couple of days ago."

Don: "No, I have some problems with the approach you took using Potter and Brumfield relays. I think you should have used Sigma relays."

Joe: (Looking at the original EWO, with directions, clearly written in Dan's hand-writing, saying that the design should be done with Potter and Brumfield relays...) "But Don, the EWO says that the design should be done with P&B relays!"

Don: "I don't care what it says, I'm the best damn engineer in the company, and I say you need to go back to the drawing boards and re-design the system to use Sigma relays"

Joe: "Ok Don. Whatever you say. (Leaving the office)"

This short exchange, in a small office in the depths of Ponderous, has a lot of different elements, all of them negative.

Why did something like this occur? Basically, because it COULD. Ponderous has created a management climate that one employee described as "the greatest concentration of control freaks in the entire state". Control is the name of the game at Ponderous. Don is demonstrating that he is in control.

Don could have legitimately changed his mind on the direction. It doesn't matter. He could not show indecision or admit any mistake. That would cause him to lose control.

Don was so far into the 'command and control' mentality, that recognizing his own handwriting required too much mental effort to perform. Don needed to use all of his efforts to maintain control of the situation.

Note also that Don thinks he is the best engineer around. Even if that had been true 10 years ago, when Don last actually did design work, it is not true now. Don has been balancing budgets, writing progress reports, writing personnel evaluations and attending management meetings for the past 10 years.

Skills not practiced atrophy. Knowledge not updated becomes stale. Lack of contact with field installation people means that he doesn't know how things are done in 'the real world' any more. In short, there is no way Don can be the best engineer any more. The key point here is that no subordinate could ever tell him that.

You see, no one who depends solely on 'control' as a measure of the stability of his or her well-being can ever deal with criticism well or fairly. The very act of being criticized implies that the 'control' manager has lost control. This is like attacking the 'food' level of Maslow's Hierarchy of Needs (Maslow, A.H., A Theory of Human Motivation,1943). A 'fight or flight' situation occurs, and believe me, a 'control freak' manager rarely flees.

What about Joe? How does he feel after this encounter? If I was into the current buzzword used by many managers without understanding, I would ask if Joe feels 'empowered'? In the previous chapter, I asked why we could only put smiles on the faces of people who were leaving. Perhaps this is one of the reasons why.

There are some who will try to argue that leaders maintain control too. That's true. However, control is generally not the main goal of a leader, and they generally use different methods to maintain control.

Somewhat trying to 'apologize' for control freaks, Cheryl Cran, in a recent book (2008) "The Control Freak Revolution: Make Your Most Maddening Behaviors Work for Your Company and to Your Advantage" may have actually categorized the control strategies of a good leader:

1. Self Control- Be constructive–observe if your actions are hurting the group, and if not, change them so that they are constructive.

2. Reality Check Control- Maintain awareness of how others see you versus how you want to be seen by them.

3. Learn and Grow Control- Keep emotions under control so you can continue to learn and grow. Realize what you are doing when you express negative emotions and pitch positive emotions instead to make the group function better.

4. Psyche Control- Try to understand the reasons why people do the things they do, even if you never are completely successful. It is the trying that is important.

5. Use Time Control instead of people control. Delegation is a form of using time control instead of

people control. It can empower people at the same time that it is saving you time.

6. Inspire people by Positive Control- Saying things in a way that is inspiring and that helps people grow maintains positive control.

7. Success Control- Make your success their success and their success your success.

Let's go on to a trap that managers and leaders both can fall into.

"The best executive is the one who has sense enough to pick good men to do what he wants done, and self-restraint enough to keep from meddling with them while they do it." - Theodore Roosevelt

"Never hire or promote in your own image. It is foolish to replicate your strength and idiotic to replicate your weakness. It is essential to employ, trust, and reward those whose perspective, ability, and judgment are radically different from yours. It is also rare, for it requires uncommon humility, tolerance, and wisdom."
- Dee W. Hock, Fast Company

CHAPTER 6

Why Humans Like Dogs

Someone once told me why humans like dogs. Dogs are professional suck-ups. They never criticize you, even when you are wrong. They fawn on your every word. Give them a crummy dog treat and they will roll over and play dead. They follow you around everywhere and act as though you were God's gift to the universe.

There is a symbiotic relationship here. The best dog suck-ups got protection from bigger animals, way more food on a regular basis, and better chances to breed. It is a survival strategy for dogs. Humans enjoy being sucked-up to. Dogs just play to that pleasure center.

The trouble is, sucking-up is a survival strategy, and 'skill' for some humans also, particularly in bureaucratic organizations. This toady or sycophant advances through the organization by sucking up to his superiors. Generally, we are not talking about a modern-day Machiavelli here. Usually, this 'skill' is developed because of a deficit somewhere else, particularly in some technical skill.

In "All Management, All the Time" organizations like Ponderous, it can give rise to dangerous levels of 'yes-men'. I once had a senior manager, in a similar organization to Ponderous, tell me that as far as he could tell, the only criterion for advancement in the organization was "to never, ever, have stated or implied that your boss was wrong".

Sycophants tell us what we want to hear. This is very comforting, but dangerous. Everyone makes mistakes. If we never hear about those mistakes, we keep on making them.

Leaders are not totally immune to suck-ups. After all, they are human. There are some self-limiting mechanisms inherent in the leadership "required conditions for existence", that tend to limit some of the potential for successful sycophancy, however.

Leadership requires a certain degree of popularity or respect. Remember, leaders cannot be appointed, they must be elected by a group of followers. Leaders or managers who succumb to the flattery of toadies begin to lose both popularity and respect after a while, as their followers and subordinates see this happening.

Would-be leaders who don't get criticized, or allow negative or implied criticisms to be voiced to them, make more mistakes, as well as lose popularity or respect or both. I remember hearing a story when I was a child about a king, I think it was Charlemagne, who went looking for the bravest man in the kingdom. The job he wanted the brave man for, was to sit behind his throne, and every time the king had to make a decision, the brave man had to whisper in the king's ear about how big a fool the king was.

Both managers and leaders need to be on the lookout for sycophants and control the urge to succumb to their blandishments. Look, it's OK to throw an occasional 'treat' to that person who tells you how wonderful you are, but the basic rules of reward and discipline should never be compromised by personal animus or favor, either.

Leadership-centered organizations also value curmudgeons. Having people who will tell you 'like it really is' serves as a valuable counter-point to the legions of people who will tell you what you want to hear.

Leaders develop 'sources' in the ranks, people they can go to for a reality check on the data they are receiving from their subordinates. This is not a source they tap on a daily basis, but one they can go to when something about the information they are receiving 'just doesn't seem right'. These generally are competent, senior contributors, who 'know where the skeletons are buried". Believe it or not, there are people like this in every organization. The key for a leader is finding them and utilizing them. This is not spying. This is listening to your followers.

Another leadership trait that helps to keep sycophants at bay, is frequently visiting the working areas of the company and talking to the people doing the work. A leader asking questions like "what would you need to be able to do your job better" accomplishes at least two things: 1) he or she demonstrates interest in what workers are doing, which just about always increases morale and 2) often gets valuable insights on what the real problems of the business are. If some intermediate manager is shorting the tool budget to pay for better office furniture for his office, it may come to light during these tours. At the very least it can offer some insights into the differences between the working level view of the business's problems, and the view of the management chain.

Well, that's enough of this topic, but before we move on, I would like to put in a shameless plug for a simple leadership behavior that I have come to miss for far too many years now.

Once a year, in an organization that I first worked for, usually at Christmas time, or in the week between Christmas and New Year's Day, the highest level manager in the building would come through the building, saying hello to everyone on the floors, and thanking them for their work over the past year. The key here was personal contact, not a group setting like a meeting. Maybe a "Happy RamaHanuKwansMas Chuck" (with apologies to Glen Beck), or a handshake with a simple 'Thank you for helping us be successful this year'. It was personal recognition, as an individual, by the leader of the group.

I know, I know, we live in a 'digital world'. Stop making excuses. If you really wanted to do something to make a personal connection with your employees, you could do it.

The medium isn't the message. The leadership is.

"Don't tell people how to do things, tell them what to do and let them surprise you with their results."
- George S. Patton

"The love of money is the root of all evil."
– 2 Thessalonians 6:10

INTERLUDE II

How Come They Don't Get It?

One of the Bible's frequent misquotes comes from the passage cited above. It is not <u>money</u> that is the root of all evil. It is the <u>love</u> of money that leads to evil doing. This is a big distinction. Nowhere is this distinction more clearly illustrated than in the world of American business today.

Let's examine such a contrast and ask ourselves how leadership principles apply.

Warren Buffet is a multi-billionaire businessman-investor. His net worth is over 30 billion dollars. Bob Baker, the CEO of Ponderous is worth considerably less than 30 billion.

Warren Buffet is considered to be the 'Wizard of Omaha', and a leader. Bob Baker is considered to be an average American corporate executive and a manager. Warren Buffet owns nearly 27% of Berkshire-Hathaway (Forbes 2009). Bob Baker owns considerably less than 1% of Ponderous.

Warren Buffet's total compensation in salary from Berkshire-Hathaway is $100,000 (Forbes 2009). Bob Baker's total compensation is $7,000,000, of which 4 million is in restricted stock and option awards.

Now let's take a look at the salary schedule for non-union employees at Ponderous.

Pay Grade	Minimum	Middle	Maximum
A	$134,000	$178,000	$222,000
B	$122,000	$162,000	$202,000
C	$110,000	$142.000	$184,000
D	$98,000	$131,000	$164,000
E	$90,000	$120,000	$149,000
F	$82,000	$109,000	$135,000
G	$73,000	$97,000	$122,000
H	$65,000	$87,000	$108,000
I	$58,000	$77,000	$108,000
J	$52,000	$69,000	$86,000
K	$46,000	$61,000	$76,000
L	$40,000	$53,000	$66,000
M	$35,000	$46,000	$57,000

What's the first thing you notice about this chart? Maybe that there is no 7 million dollar range? Well that's because at the VP level and above, the salary schedule isn't published, at least to the employees. Those figures show up in obfuscated fashion in 10-K and annual reports to the stockholders. If the publication wasn't required by law, no one might ever see the figures.

If you mathematically analyze the chart, you might note that moving upwards between pay grades starts out at about 15% at the lower levels and gradually goes down to about 10% or less at the higher levels.

In order to move up to the levels of top executives' salaries, it is obvious from the chart that you have to have salary increases in multiple hundreds of percent to get to those levels. Using the mid-range values, Bob Baker is making over 150 times what the lowest-level management employee is making at Ponderous.

Why is this? Warren Buffet and Charlie Munger were recently quoted at the Berkshire-Hathaway shareowners meeting:

We think we have a good system.

Your question implies that the board sets these things. In the recent forty years, basically the board has had little effect on these things. The CEO has had an important role determining their compensation. These people pick their own compensation committee. I've been on one compensation committee out of nineteen boards because these people aren't looking for Dobermans; they're looking for cocker spaniels. It's been a system that the CEO has dominated. In my experience, boards have done little in the way of thinking through as an owner what they ought to pay these people.

Here in town, Pete Kiewit figured out a very logical way to pay people in his business. It's not rocket science--you would be able to figure it out, I can figure it out, but you have to understand that not every CEO wants a rational compensation committee.

I don't think there should be a compensation committee...
It can be done. It's very difficult to have a system where the board, thinking as owners, care as much as the guy on the other side of the negotiating table. But it's very important how you compensate the CEO, and it can be done.

Charlie Munger added:

Liberally paid boards of directors can be counterproductive. There's a sort of reciprocation--you keep raising me, and I keep raising you, and it's very clublike. (Megan McArdle, Asymmetrical Information Blog)

Members of the Board of Directors at Ponderous are paid over $100,000 a year for their 'service'. In the 2006 Berkshire-Hathaway annual shareholder letter, Warren Buffet addressed Director compensation in this context:

In selecting a new director [Yahoo! CFO Susan Decker], we were guided by our long-standing criteria, which are that board members be owner-oriented, business-savvy, interested and truly independent. I say "truly" because many directors who are now deemed independent by various authorities and observers are far from that, relying heavily as they do on directors' fees to maintain their standard of living. These payments, which come in many forms, often range between $150,000 and $250,000 annually, compensation that may approach or even exceed all other income of the "independent" director. And – surprise, surprise – director compensation has soared in recent years, pushed up by recommendations from corporate America's favorite consultant, Ratchet, Ratchet and Bingo. (The name may be phony, but the action it conveys is not.)

Charlie and I believe our four criteria are essential if directors are to do their job – which, by law, is to faithfully represent owners. Yet these criteria are usually ignored. Instead, consultants and CEOs seeking board candidates will often say, "We're looking for a woman," or "a Hispanic," or "someone from abroad," or what have you. It sometimes sounds as if the mission is to stock Noah's ark. Over the years I've been queried many times about potential directors and have yet to hear anyone ask, "Does he think like an intelligent owner?"

So why are people mad at Bob Baker for his salary, and not at Warren Buffet, one of the world's richest men? Fairness.

The American obsession with fairness is built into the character of the country. Whether you refer to life as a game, a competition, a level playing field on which everyone gains by their own merits, or even as a journey whose destination is never fixed, the idea is that anything that changes the rules to unjustly favor one of the participants outside of their own efforts and random chance should not be allowed.

Once you have convinced Americans that something is not 'fair', you have created a political fulcrum that you can leverage to change laws and policies nearly anywhere you want. Again, as Warren Buffet pointed out when asked about Congress' threat to enact a 90% 'bonus tax' on bonuses paid to AIG executives:

> "That was uncontrolled fury. They just wanted to do something, and they did it. They still want to do something, maybe not something that spectacular, but Berkshire Hathaway will be affected by some of this"

The public was furious, and Congress felt the heat. The fury was driven by the general sense that the bonuses were unfair. Contracts be damned.

The reason that the majority of these paragons of business, the CEO's, CFO's, CIO's, the "C-level" executives that salesmen and consultants covet to contact, don't 'get it', is that most of them are managers, not leaders.

Managers don't think in terms of having to convince followers (or the public) that they deserve what they are getting in compensation. People don't mind someone like Warren Buffet, who takes a modest salary and grows his business to make his investment in that business worth more, making lots of money. That, after all, is the 'American Dream'.

What they <u>do</u> mind is mercenaries, who come in, demand the money up front, and who, whether their companies win or lose, come out with a pile of guaranteed money. Mercenaries have talent. Mercenaries have vision. Mercenaries can direct organizations effectively. They are still mercenaries.

Blather on all you want to, about market forces, compensation committees appraising the situations, comparables to other executives in other companies, or even to the salaries of baseball players. You've missed the point, managers of America. You're NOT leaders.

"Mercenary - (n.) One who is hired; a hireling; especially, a soldier hired into foreign service. (a.) Hence: Moved by considerations of pay or profit; greedy of gain; sordid; selfish. (a.) Acting for reward; serving for pay; paid; hired; hireling; venal; as, mercenary soldiers".
Thinkexist.com

"Mushroom management is an allusion to a company's staff being treated like mushrooms: kept in the dark, covered with dung, and—when grown big enough— canned. The connotation is that the management is making decisions without consulting the staff affected by those decisions—and possibly not even informing the staff until well after such decisions are made." –Wikipedia

CHAPTER 7

Death of a Thousand Emails

Ling Chi, the 'death of a thousand cuts', was a form of corporal punishment used in China for nearly a thousand years. It provided a slow and lingering death. The metaphor of a "death of a thousand cuts' is often used symbolically to describe the incremental destruction of something.

The use and misuse of email is inflicting the 'death of a thousand cuts' on leadership opportunities and skills in American business today. It has been reported that the typical knowledge-worker in a Fortune 500 company receives an average of 150 emails a day. If you assume an average of one minute per email to deal with or respond to each message, two and a half hours of every business day is being spent answering email.

Don't get me wrong. Email can be a godsend in some situations. It allows time-shifting. It puts things in writing for future documentation. It is quick (usually) and (mostly) convenient. It enables a lot of workflow functionality in business.

It can also provide a lot of evidence and laughs when it is made public. Just go to a website like www.enronemail.com where you can search and read more than 500,000 internal emails discovered in the litigation surrounding the Enron collapse.

It has also enabled a lot of managers to make mistakes at warp speed, particularly in areas of leadership behavior. What seems to be forgotten is that there is a person at the other end of that email, and that person deserves to be led as well as managed.

We could start off with the simplest rules, like "Don't put anything in an email that you wouldn't want your mother to be reading in the paper the next day", or for those for whom shame isn't enough "Don't put anything in an email that you wouldn't want to be explaining in court on the witness stand".

Those may be interpreted by some as dealing more with 'how' something is said. In truth, there is that, but more to the point, there are some subjects that should NOT be put in emails, particularly for the first contact to an employee on something that is personal, or vital to their well-being.

Prime example. Anyone who fires an employee via an email is neither a leader, nor a manager. They are a jerk. They are cowardly. They are a lot of <unprintable> things. This will be true 99.44% of the time, no matter what excuses are offered for doing it. Your excuse is probably not in the .56% category either. Laying them off by phone is a distant second, classless enough, but not rising to the level of the email version.

Another caveat I would offer is that with the state of email today, corporate monitoring systems, address books, and distribution lists proliferating mean that you probably should treat every email as though you were going to grab a megaphone and broadcast the message over your cubicle wall to the rest of the organization. Don't believe me? How many times have you seen some stupid reply broadcast to the entire organization because someone hit 'Reply All' to an email with a broadcast distribution list? Don't think the next such mistake couldn't be yours.

What is causing email to trend toward being a torture system rather than a performance enhancer?

Lack of a leadership perspective on the design of the emails, and usage of the email systems.

Leaders would inherently understand that the systems utilizing email should serve the users. The users aren't there to serve the systems. Managers get most of these systems built, however, and they look at them through the old lenses of planning, organization, staffing, direction and control. These management email systems exist to get information management wants to convey to the workers. That is not exactly the same thing as conveying the information that the workers need to receive in order to do their jobs.

From a leadership perspective, you would start at the worker and ask what they needed to do their job, and then build a system to supply that information.

Let's go into the Ponderous email system and see what we get. Here's a sample:

From: RoboMail@ponderous.com
Sent: Wednesday, July 16, 2008 8:17 AM
To: IT Department (3 0r 4 Hundred People)
Subject: BM14955\PROBLEM OPENED: Ponderous.net Printers - Printing problems - Customer Reported

Problem: OPENED BM14955
OPENED Date/Time: July 16, 2008 08:16 AM
Asset: Ponderous.net Printers
Problem: Printing problems
Reported by: Customer

{Here is an automated system sending out an email to several hundred people, who now know that somewhere on a network of 10,000 users and a thousand servers, there is some problem with printing, reported by someone. About the only actionable item in this email is the problem ticket number, which could be used to go in manually to an information system that MIGHT contain actionable information. Why doesn't this message have enough information for the average intelligent reader to make a decision as to whether or not this might be something they have to do something about or with?}

From: RoboMail@ponderous.com
Sent: Tuesday , 07/15/08 15:36
To: IT Department (3 0r 4 Hundred People)
07/15/08 15:36:12: Incident BM14942 has been opened and assigned to your group.
The following Incident has been assigned to your group for resolution:
Incident #: BM149472 Ticket Status:
Please do not reply to this message.

This email account is not monitored for inbound mail.

{yeah, I wouldn't want to receive replies to THIS either}

Incident Details
Alert Status: Assigned Group: Technical Services
Category: automated events Assigned to:
Subcategory: abc Severity: 3
Software Type: Contact's Phone:
Problem Type: Contact's Location:
Contact: Joe Operator User ID:
CC#: Asset's Location:
Email: Region:
Reported By: Reporter's Phone:
Asset ID:: server-bs-1
Incident Description
server-bs-1-   IS_Down   server-bs-1_ponderous_com:6969 - 2 intervals of 0.0 compare.equalTo 0.0 (Tue Jul 15 15:30:09 EDT 2008)
AI - webShlep Infrastructure Component Failure - Call out

{Again note that we have an automated email system sending out emails to possibly dozens of people, only one or two of which actually can do anything to resolve the situation. The recipients are presented with practically no information, despite the appearance of multiple fields that could contain information, but don't. If you saw something like this

73

on your personal email account, you would call it
SPAM. You do learn that 0=0, however.}

The too-often used buzzword "artificial intelligence" by its very nature, implies the existence of "artificial stupidity". I personally have observed more instances of the latter than of the former, in these types of automated email systems.

So, where is the leadership failure?

It is in not understanding what information is needed to respond to a problem, or perform a task, and then compounding the problem by not insisting that systems be programmed to provide actionable information to the subordinates that will receive them. The important thing is NOT getting a directive out to the troops. The important thing is getting information targeted to your team to enable them to do their job quicker and with better quality.

Setting up automated systems to notify people without these considerations is like being proud of being able to shoot a machine gun while blindfolded. There is a feeling of power with all the noise and recoil, and you can hear bullets flying everywhere, so you know your 'message' is getting 'out'. What you don't see is all the ducking and dodging going on around you and the chaos you are causing.

There is also a very, very, old maxim of human factors engineering that comes into play here – Never, ever, design a system that is going to be alarming all the time, particularly if the vast majority of the 'alarms' don't require very specific actions to resolve. After a very short time, humans will naturally acclimatize themselves to the alarms and begin ignoring many of them.

What you want is a system that is silent until something actionable occurs. You want the alarm to be specific, actionable and to give the responder sufficient information to judge the severity and a context for where to go to get enough information to deal with the problem.

We could stop slicing up our employees with email 'bullets', if managers applied these principles to all automated email systems, using a leadership viewpoint. Just because it is cheaper and faster to program systems to detect a problem and send out a generic message, leaving the recipient to sort out the response required, doesn't mean we should do things that way. So why do we?

And that subject, why American business does things the way they do, will lead us on to the topic of training.

> *"A competent leader can get efficient service from poor troops, while on the contrary an incapable leader can demoralize the best of troops."*
> *- General of the Armies John J. Pershing*

Emails Have More Lives Than A Cat

- Read emails twice before you send them and use a spell-checker
- Be sensitive about how you say things in an email – don't say things you would be punched in the nose for saying if you were face-to-face
- Don't encourage 'flame wars' (Don't reply in anger immediately)
- Avoid the use of Reply All to every message
- Don't copy emails to someone's boss as a means to force them to do something
- Don't email anything, including words, that you would be embarrassed to explain in public

"The ultimate leader is one who is willing to develop people to the point that they eventually surpass him or her in knowledge and ability."
- Fred A. Manske, Jr.

CHAPTER 8

"Training??? We Don't Need No Stinking Training"

There is a misconception in much of American business that most training, particularly 'outside' training, is some kind of boondoggle. It is something that is more of a work perk, not a necessity, and much of it is just attended to get to go visit some interesting place. You can see this attitude in places where managers are required to have 'training' budgets, and those are the first items that get chopped when the call comes out to tighten belts.

Part of this lack of consideration for training comes from the remarkably short-term view that much of American business has adopted by merely focusing on 'the bottom line'. You don't get any sense of long-term, strategic thinking in most American businesses today. What you get is the belief that if something doesn't contribute to earnings per share this year or next, it isn't very valuable.

It's that way at Ponderous too. It goes deeper than just cutting training when things get tough though. There is no appreciation for what training can be used for to strengthen the organization. Joe Risingstar, a young engineer, has just been promoted to the job of group lead. For the first time in his career, Joe will have to deal with corporate infrastructure and systems, like budgeting and finance. He goes to his boss, Tom Deacon, for advice:

Joe: "Hey Tom, gotta minute?"

Tom: (shuffling a pile of papers on his desk) "I've got 5 minutes before I have to be in my next meeting. What do you want?"

Joe: "Well, your clerk just dropped off these budget spreadsheets with all these budget categories. I haven't got a clue what to do with them?"

Tom: "I don't really have time to go over the whole budget process with you. I'm tied up all week in meetings. See if you can get with one of the other group leads and have them try to explain it to you. If that doesn't work, look at my schedule and try to find an hour when we can sit down and I'll try to explain them to you".

Joe: "Well, I've tried talking to the other group leads, and they all have different ideas about what the categories are for, and besides, they are too busy to have much time to talk to me. Is there a manual from Finance on how to fill these things out, or some training on the system I could go to?"

Tom: "Finance is too busy to do more than put together some procedures for their own use, let alone try to make their process clear to people outside the department. I had to learn everything I know about the system by trial and error. Training is a waste of time, it just takes you away from productive work. I've got to leave for my meeting. Just do the best you can with those spreadsheets".

Poor Joe. This isn't going to be the only time he is left out to dry. He has never supervised another person before, and there is nowhere in Ponderous that he can turn to for training in the nitty-gritty policies and procedures that a supervisor needs to know at Ponderous. There are some 'polishing' courses, like how to be a better speaker and how to make better presentation slides. Maybe he can go to a community college on his own time and take some management classes...

The problem is, no one at Ponderous has ever created a shared vision of what a Ponderous supervisor should be, or how a supervisor should act. So, people learn by watching their supervisor. If that supervisor is a son-of-a-bitch, then the assumption is that you have to be an SOB to be a supervisor. No one in the company ever is put to the test to validate that assumption, because there is nothing to test against. No one can point to any training or documentation that even says what is expected of a supervisor or manager of Ponderous. Sure, there are '40,000 foot' things like Visions, Ethics and Values statements, but nothing at the ground level. There just is no common expectation of any Ponderous supervisor.

There is a thus a great deal of emphasis on watching what the person above you is doing, and slavishly trying to emulate that. Many 'decisions' at Ponderous are accomplished by trying to successfully guess what position the person above you holds on the subject. There are a lot of 'rear-enders' when the Ponderous CEO stops suddenly, in other words.

Contrast that with another Fortune 500 company, General Electric. My introduction to GE was the "A-B-C program", now I believe called the "Edison Engineering program". As an engineer, fresh out of college, I was invited to learn how GE wanted its engineers to perform their work. For the first three years of my career with GE, I rotated every 6 months to another job, in another area of my division, as a 'program engineer'. You might think of it as sort of an internship on steroids.

In order to keep with the program, I had to devote up to 20 hours a week of my own time to attend classes held at work, and do assigned homework, being taught by experienced GE engineers, on how to do 'real' work. There was a carrot – in the third year, I would be sent to get my Master's degree, at GE's expense, at a 'local' university (UC Berkeley). GE got engineers that knew the 'GE way' of doing things. I got a Master's degree.

The real point of this is that GE also had similar programs for managers. These programs also didn't wait until you actually became a manager. If you were selected as having 'potential' by your supervisor, you would be started down a track of learning that developed you as a potential 'GE supervisor'. There was a common expectation of what a GE supervisor was expected to know, and how they were supposed to act. If cultural change or legal change occurred (think 'Women's Rights'), there was training provided in how the company expected a 'GE manager' to deal with it.

This is not a new phenomenon. In 1954, GE published a set of four 9x12" books of about 250 pages apiece, entitled "Professional Management in General Electric". Ralph J. Cordiner, the President of GE, wrote an introduction "To all General Electric Managers and other Professional Employees:"

> *"The growth of the General Electric Company over the past 75 years has been the result of planning and design. Periodically, the Company has demonstrated its ability to expand in relation to the demands made upon it by a rapidly growing economy and by an even more rapidly growing electrical industry. In these periods of change and expansion, the Company has demonstrated a unique quality of organizational flexibility–a quality that has allowed the business not only to adopt but to take advantage of changing conditions in our social, political and economic life. Our period of greatest growth still lies ahead. As forward-looking manager we must be prepared to meet the problems that come with increased size and complexity. It is essential, therefore, that we plan to preserve the advantages of industrial greatness and at the same time <u>avoid the tendency toward bureaucracy, which inhibits future growth and which stifles individual initiative</u>." {emphasis added}*

As I write this, the paragraph above was written 55 years ago. Leaving out the growth references as historical, the principles of organizational flexibility created by managers trained to lead as well as manage, are still just as valid today as they ever were.

Yes, I said <u>managers</u> trained to lead. In book 3 of "Professional Management at General Electric – The Work of a Professional Manager" the heading of page 186 is "The Ability to Lead Can Be Learned"

> *"Unquestionably, some individuals show attributes of leadership very early in their personal growth. They have ideas and plans which make sense to others. They have beliefs, energy and emotional drive which prompts them to strongly promote such ideas and plans and which engender confidence in others that the plans are worth following...*
>
> *The thesis at this point is that one can learn how to be an effective leader, and that those who continue to be leaders among us have learned and have consciously exercised practices which result in voluntary following of such leadership by others."*

There has to be a commitment on the part of both sides. A commitment to train and a commitment to learn. The basic lack of any commitment in American business to either will be explored next.

"The way to miss success is to miss the opportunity." -
Victor Chasles

Why Training Is Important

Start with a cage containing five monkeys. Inside the cage, hang a banana on a string and place a set of stairs under it. Before long, a monkey will go to the stairs and start to climb towards the banana. As soon as he touches the stairs, spray all of the other monkeys with cold water. After a while, another monkey makes an attempt with the same result—all the other monkeys are sprayed with cold water. Pretty soon, when another monkey tries to climb the stairs, the other monkeys will try to prevent it.

Now, put away the cold water. Remove one monkey from the cage and replace it with a new one. The new monkey sees the banana and wants to climb the stairs. To his surprise and horror, all of the other monkeys attack him. After another attempt and attack, he knows that if he tries to climb the stairs, he will be assaulted.

Next, remove another of the original five monkeys and replace it with a new one. The newcomer goes to the stairs and is attacked. The previous newcomer takes part in the punishment with enthusiasm! Likewise, replace a third original monkey with a new one, then a fourth, then the fifth. Every time the newest monkey takes to the stairs, he is attacked. Most of the monkeys that are beating him have no idea why they were not permitted to climb the stairs or why they are participating in the beating of the newest monkey. After replacing all the original monkeys, none of the remaining monkeys have ever been sprayed with cold water. Nevertheless, no monkey ever again approaches the stairs to try for the banana. –Michael Michalko

Why not? Because as far as they know that's the way it's always been done around here, and that is how company policy begins.

85

INTERLUDE III

What Happened to Jerry?

All of us working in the Fortune 500 have had this experience. One day, we are working for someone, or with someone, and the next day they are gone, just disappeared. Then there is the carefully worded internal memo.

"Jerry has retired from Ponderous. We wish him well in his retirement". Of course, Jerry has only been with the company a few years, and is usually nowhere near normal retirement age. Jerry is usually a high level manager or executive brought in from another company, and usually has a contract with some form of golden parachute just for such an occasion.

Then there is the ever-popular "Jerry has left to pursue other opportunities" If you are a friend of Jerry's, and happen to ask him what those 'opportunities' are, you may find that they haven't really presented themselves yet.

Corporate America really doesn't like to air its dirty laundry in public. I suppose you can't really blame them with all the lawyers out there ready to sue if you drop your hat. So, you have these mystery departures from the corporate scene.

My observation is that many of these departures are part of an all-too-common occurrence in corporate America today, the deliberate destruction of natural leaders in the organization. You see, nothing is more threatening to a non-leader manager, than a natural leader below him, or at the same level, competing for the next promotion.

When there is a natural leader in an organization, people in the organization tend to act in ways that threaten managers' power bases. When a real leader is chosen for a new team, people line up to join the team. When a pure manager is chosen to take on such a task, volunteers are just not to be found.

A leader can get the volunteers he needs for an assignment, a pure manager never asks for any because he knows it would be wasting his time. So a natural leader may have all the help he needs on his or her projects, while others in the organization are struggling to get their jobs done because "people aren't cooperating". This situation often leads to jealousy and frustration.

When 'things are going on' or there are rampant rumors about some major shift at the company, people often turn to natural leaders in an organization, that are not their managers, for advice and counsel. This often infuriates managers. If those managers have military experience, the phrase most often used is "going outside the chain of command" in these situations.

If you are 'feeling lucky' as Dirty Harry would say, and want to see a fast way to infuriate your 'command and control' manager, just let yourself be seen having a close conversation with one of his peers for a number of minutes without your manager being invited. You know, you might be giving away the secret defense plans for the next revision of the company budget.

Being a person with leadership ability in a manager-controlled organization is risky business. Managers, particularly that 'command and control' type previously mentioned, feel threatened by natural leaders. For one thing, the control of the group is in question if people turn to a natural leader within the group instead of looking to the manager for all guidance. Maintaining. control is right there on the base of Mazlow's pyramid with food and shelter for these managers. It's 'fight or flight', baby.

Now if a leader is a peer with other managers, they can be done in by lack of skill in corporate in-fighting. The art of bureaucracy is a management, not a leadership skill. A person with leadership skills, especially one brought in from outside the company, can be at a distinct disadvantage in a corporate environment that hasn't espoused leadership as an important skill previously.

A corporate bureaucrat, sensing a leader as a threat to his or her position, can subtly steer the unknowing leader into questioning company policies that are known to be 'sensitive' to upper management, or undermine the leader's credibility by 'mentioning' that the leader seems to be 'too sympathetic to employee concerns rather than the needs of the company', or that the leader is letting 'his people get out of control', playing on known fears of a command and control CEO. It can be worked many ways.

Since leaders 'stick out' in many ways, they are also subject to the bureaucratic maxim that you don't want to be the tallest blade of grass. That is the one that is always hit by the lawnmower first. So, if a 'kick ass and take names' command and control organization is looking for someone to kick, often leaders, particularly ones not sponsored from the top, having come up through the ranks, are primary targets.

Another pitfall for a leader is in coming into an organization from the outside, without complete understanding of the culture you are coming into. Often, leaders are tempted by offers to come into an organization to 'create change' and 'bring in new blood'. This has a chance of being true and work if the very top of the organization is trying to create a new environment, and actually wants change to occur. If you are coming into a command and control organizational culture, in the middle management ranks, without that top-down support, however, you could find yourself in about the same situation as taking an A-positive transfusion into a B-negative body. DOA. I saw one manager survive about a year in such a situation, and believe me, it wasn't pretty. Et tu Brutus, eh Marcus?

Human organisms and organizations are resistant to change. The change management process is difficult enough without having the extra burden of a philosophical war between leaders and managers. Be sure you know what you are getting into before parachuting into a company. Ask some employees what goes on in the organization. Every organization has at least one curmudgeon who will tell you 'how it really works'. Finding that person can be a sanity-preserver if it lets you avoid being a casualty of the war between leadership and managership.

For this whole trend of leadership denigration to be reversed, corporate America needs to understand that efficient organization alone will not be sufficient to compete in a world economy. Increased leadership content will be required to get people to 'go the extra mile'.

In his hard-hitting presentation "Did you Know…?"*, school technologist Karl Fisch pointed out:

- If you're one in a million in China…There are 1,300 people just like you.
- In India, there are 1,100 people just like you.
- The 25% of the population in China with the highest IQ's…Is greater than the total population of North America.
- In India, it's the top 28%.

- Translation for teachers: They have more honors kids than we have kids.
- China will soon become the number one English speaking country in the world.
- If you took every single job in the U.S. today and shipped it to China...China would still have a labor surplus.

We have a tough road ahead of us and we need leadership, not just managership, to make it. Stop trying to get rid of it.

*Go to www.YouTube.com and search for Did You Know.

"Good leaders believe that every team member matters and foster an environment that makes everyone feel important. It is no wonder they attract all the support they need to help them achieve their goals." – Tag Goulet

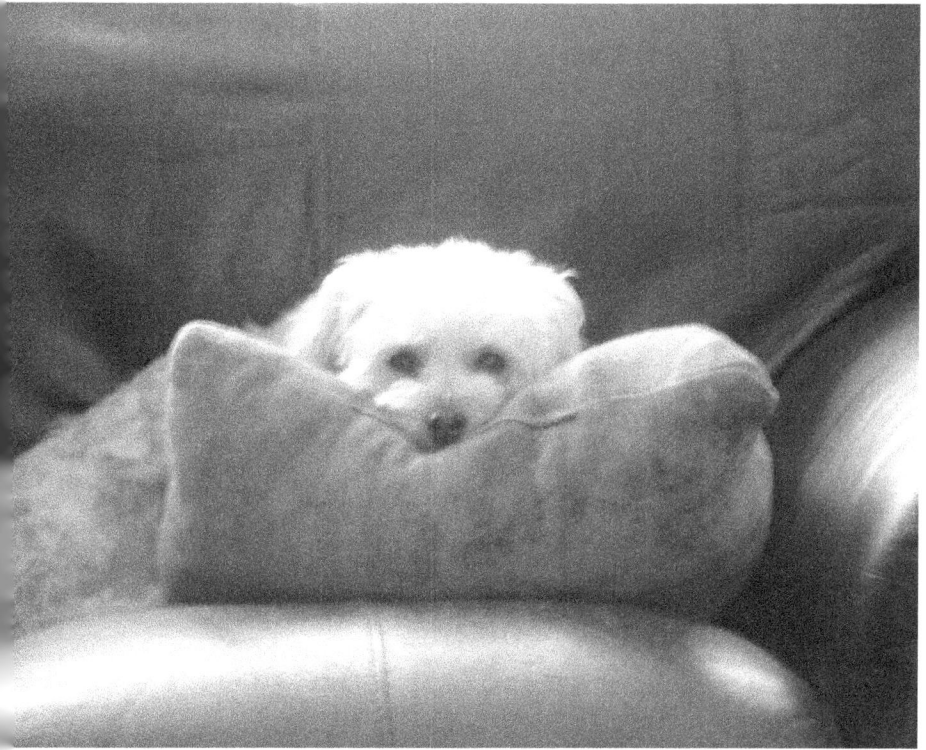

"For all sad words of tongue and pen, The
saddest are these, 'It might have been'."
– John Greenleaf Whittier

"Good leaders make people feel that they're at the very heart of things, not at the periphery. Everyone feels that he or she makes a difference to the success of the organization. When that happens people feel centered and that gives their work meaning."
- Warren Bennis

CHAPTER 9

How Did We Get Where We Are Now?

There are many diverse factors that have driven leadership from the American business scene. Technology has played a part. But there are sociological, demographic, propaganda and mercenary effects that have had a role also.

In the first part of the 20th century, the concept of 'scientific management' evolved. Scientific discoveries were accelerating and the impact of science on everyday life was increasing. It was not much of a leap of faith to believe that managing could be made more 'scientific'. Managing dealt with facts that could be observed, classified, organized and arranged into a systemized body of knowledge.

Facts are always easier to deal with than people. There were a lot of fact-based problems in management that could be dealt with through the increased rigor of scientific thought processes. So, scientific management could initially provide improvements in American business. The problem is that 'scientific leadership' wasn't being pursued at the same time.

There were some cautionary notes:

1. There is a foundation for a true "science of managing": One which will be invariate and one whose principles derive from a higher level that the changing forces and pressures of the current social matrix; and One which can be stated, verified, taught and used as a process in which the principles themselves can be applied to mold the results of the enterprise in spite of the social pressures impinging.

2. Such a true "science of managing" is rooted in: The principles of liberty, not in the principles of compulsion; the principles of reason, not in the principles of force; the principles of leadership by integration of voluntary individual efforts in co-operative teamwork, and not in the principles of command, control or dictation; and therefore in, the principles of morality, not in the principles of materialism; The principles of religion, not in the principles of atheism; and finally in, The deep belief that, however complex society and its social inter-relationships may become, the natural rights of the individual, as a person, including the right to acquire and to hold property, are of a higher order of priority than all of the other rights in the so-called social matrix; and in the recognition that if such other rights are to have validity or permancency, they must themselves flow from initial, voluntary agreement of the individuals concerned to modify the maintenance of their full personal liberties for their mutual, or collective security or benefit." Pp 143-144, "The Work of a Professional Manager", General Electric Company, 1954.

So, what did we get? A lot of slick methods for increasing managerial effectiveness:

- Project Management and PERT charts
- Spreadsheets and Accounting programs
- Industrial Engineering and Time and Motion Studies

- Inventory Management and Just in Time Manufacturing
- Kepner-Tregoe™ Problem Solving
- Workflow and Business Process Management

To name but a few. Notice that none of these techniques have anything much to do with interacting with people. That is, with the leadership aspect of the equation:

$$People + Processes = Work$$

Because of the emphasis on 'scientific' method and analysis, the type of person most artful in (and therefore attracted to) the management schemes spawned by late-20th century 'scientific management' tended to be what I call "Hoovers". They wanted to suck those pesky human-interaction problems out of their neat schemes for controlling their world. Leadership didn't seem to have a place in their bright and shiny view of a modern business. Managers started to believe all the propaganda about how better management could improve business.

This led further to the concept of the Replaceable Employee Unit (REU). The concept of the REU fit in neatly into analyses and spreadsheets. If you needed work done, you just plugged in so many REU's to get the job done. You wouldn't have to factor in any variability, because one REU was just the same as another, right?

All REU's of the same job classification do the same amount of work, so they all should be paid the same, right? It makes it so much easier doing the budget forecasts.

In REU-land, there is no such thing as an 'expert' REU. If one REU leaves by 'attrition', you just replace that unit with another. Or, better yet, spread the workload amongst the remaining REU's, who all know how to do the same work, right. Helps the bottom line every time. (And you wondered where the concept of salary 'midpoints' came from).

Sociological pressures didn't help the trend toward trying to eliminate the people variability factor. Changing demographics and workplace diversity increases meant that leadership-challenged managers had even more problems to deal with. In a defensive posture already, the temptation of the REU approach was the siren's song to many managers, and though they tried to hide it, their actions spoke louder than words.

Ponderous Power and Light had a sense that employees didn't understand the new competitive environment that the company was facing with de-regulation of the electric power industry, and so it decided to have a company-wide meeting that would involve 1000 or so selected employees from all divisions who could hear the message and relate it back to their fellow employees.

Ponderous was having a tough set of negotiations with their main union at the same time, and it was with some reluctance that upper management agreed that all levels of employees should be represented in this important meeting.

The meeting was held in a large public auditorium. Company speakers, from the chief financial officer, to the Washington, DC, federal affairs manager, spoke on what was happening with deregulation and how it was going to affect Ponderous. Finally, the CEO and Chairman of the Board, John Whuthe, ended the presentations with a speech on how the entire company was going to have to pull together to make it through the trying times ahead. He then opened up the floor for questions. After the usual couple of softball questions posed by mid-level managers at such meetings, a union lineman approached the microphone wearing his leather union jacket.

'John, what are you going to do to preserve jobs during all of this? You are bargaining with us, but you aren't talking to us. John, employees are not your enemy, please don't treat us that way!'

One thousand sets of eyes focused on the CEO at that moment. What did they see? They saw a frozen-faced man staring out toward the far side of the auditorium, not looking at the man who asked the question. The eye position never changed as John responded.

What employees heard was a set of words that really didn't answer anything. Particularly, they didn't hear any response directly to the union man, nor to the underlying plea not to consider employees the enemy. Right then, the majority of people there were convinced that they WERE the enemy.

A leader would have known that he could not leave behind any implication with his followers that he considered them the 'enemy'. In the land of REU's, anyone who doesn't follow the program or agree automatically with the management direction, often is viewed as the enemy.

Technology has not helped much, either, as noted before. By allowing for fast communications without having to interface with anyone to establish a connection (emails, text-messaging) it allows managers who don't like personal interactions to hide behind an electronic veil. Telecommuting diminishes much personal contact with your boss and co-workers. Managers can almost imagine that they are sending orders to robotic units in a factory of the future.

Mistakes can be made almost at the speed of light. It used to be that the personal note you scribbled on that memo might be only found by the person emptying your wastebasket. Now it only takes one click on "Reply All" to send your pithy comment all through the company.

Faceless interaction with electronic screens instead of persons leads to current social phenomena like 'flame wars', 'lurkers', acid-blogs and anonymous outrageous comments on newsgroups and article-response blogs. Civility used to be a product of either culture, learning, or fear that you would get poked in the nose. Technology has removed one of those restraints of civilization.

Demographics have played a part in allowing part of the leadership vacuum to develop also. The last half of the 20th century was the realm of the baby-boomers. Raised by depression-surviving parents, heirs to the world after World War II, they were shaped by many factors, including the Cold War and the threat of nuclear annihilation. They started out with a work ethic that dedicated themselves possibly more to their jobs than their families.

Over the course of the work history of this generation, the ascendency of managership over leadership has 'progressed' to the point where many boomers are disaffected with working conditions. They have seen workloads increase without corresponding remuneration, expertise and skill devalued and less and less communication TO them while communications ABOUT them increase. They are disaffected, and plan on leaving jobs in droves over the next few years.

This coincides with another generation, X-ers, coming into ascendancy. Their generation is smaller in size than the boomers, and they have much different attitudes about work. Many current managers will be disappointed to learn that Generation X believes that they actually do have a life outside of work, and that they don't believe that they will or have to work for the same company all their life.

These demographics and sociological changes mean that managers who have been able to get by without leadership behaviors are going to be seriously challenged in the future. In addition, society in general would benefit from more real leadership being available.

The natural question is, then, WHAT DO WE DO ABOUT
THIS MESS?

> *"Leadership is a combination of strategy and character.*
> *If you must be without one, be without the strategy." -*
> *Gen. H. Norman Schwarzkopf*

"MOREL" MUSHROOMS.

Rexford Ballard 1916

*"Recognize Difficult People as they are. Stop hoping
they'll miraculously change or disappear."*
– Coping with Difficult People, Robert M. Branson, PhD

CHAPTER 10

So What Do We Do Now?

So sociologic and technology trends are devaluing the concept of leadership in American business. Do we have to stand by and let that happen? Can leadership make a difference? I say hell no we don't and hell yes it can. Leadership can make the difference between an adequately-performing organization (managed) and a top-performing organization (led).

I can't tell you how much talent I have seen wasted over the years because of internal power struggles in manager-dominated organizations. This is wasted talent that could be utilized with just a small amount of applied leadership. If you don't think that the lust to dominate other people is a prime motivator, you have never been in an organization managed by control freaks, like Ponderous Power & Light.

It doesn't take a wholesale replacement of today's business managers to change this situation. We can create a business culture where leadership behaviors are modeled and valued. Eventually, it is true, that we need to create more leaders who can manage. Right now, the state of affairs is so bad that we can get marked improvements by simply creating more people who can MANAGE to APPEAR to lead. This is because the **appearance** of having some leadership in most companies is more real leadership than they have now.

My contention is that most managers, particularly early in their management careers, could be taught to model leadership behaviors. In most cases, it would not matter to followers if their 'leader' was acting from skill and innovative thinking, or simply 'acting', as in the theater, if the behaviors the followers saw were those of a leader.

Another way of saying this is that the ability to lead can be learned, at least to a point of understanding the practices of leadership. In 1954, General Electric, in the book "Professional Management in General Electric" stated their management's vision of the practices of a leader by contrasting "The Leader" to "The Dominator" in the chart, "A Professional Manager Leads Rather Than Commands":

The Leader	The Dominator
Serves the Common Need	Serves Own Needs
Informs and Inspires	Drives
Depends on Authority	Depends on Imposed Power
Depends on Goodwill	Depends on Force
Inspires Enthusiasm	Inspires Fear
Says : "WE"	Says: "I"
Says : "LET'S GO"	Says: "GO"
Develops Successor	Develops Himself
Plays with "TEAM"	"GRANDSTANDS"

If you took this chart and rated your supervisors and managers on the two columns of characteristics, what would you see? Would your organization be like the gang from Ponderous who went to the local Chinese management restaurant and picked everything from "Column B"?

So, what can we train managers to do that will make them appear to be leaders? While some of these techniques (and attitudes) might sound just like manipulation, the idea is that if you get people to support you willingly, you get the best results.

A. Treat EVERYONE with justice and respect. This is a principle that is found in just about every major world religion and philosophy. It is hard to find a more succinct statement of this "Golden Rule" than in the King James Bible verse Luke 6:31 "And as ye would that men should do to you, do ye also to them likewise". It is not rocket science.

You communicate your belief that every person is important by remembering to greet and introduce people by their preferred names (and YES, you should know what that is if they work for you), and never refer to them as "subordinates".

B. Treat your direct reports and people that work for them, or are lower than you are on the corporate ladder, as people you have to convince to go with you, not someone you can order to go to the place where you want them to go.

Just as not every order has to be reacted to within a few milliseconds to accomplish the goals of an organization, not every order can be free of any explanation. Try to offer a rationale and a context whenever you can.

C. Consider as one of the first steps in any decision process, the impact on and appearance to, your subordinates, of any order or decision that you intend to give or convey to them. Address what they will think of you and the company when they hear what you have to say and how you say it.

Get in the habit of doing this even for routine matters, so it will be second-nature for the really important ones. Tailor the manner in which you present the matter to address the issues you know will arise. Thoughtless command and control is the surest way to lower your apparent IQ.

D. The rules are the rules for EVERYBODY. That includes everyone from the janitor to the CEO.

At Ponderous, the building department has an undocumented rule that they will never start a fire drill when Bob Baker is in the headquarters building. It doesn't matter whether Bob told them to do that or not. If you have a business culture that is doing that kind of thinking at ANY level, it is bad for the organization.

Think of what messages this kind of situation could be sending to the organization:

Bob Baker's time is more valuable than any other person in the organization. (Might not be true the day an energy trader misses out on a sweet deal because he had to evacuate the trading floor at an inopportune time)

Do as I say, not as I do. (A quick way to get a corporation into trouble is to have someone think that only the people below them have to comply with regulations, like Sarbanes-Oxley)

Rules are only for those who need a lot of direction, the subordinates. (Americans really HATE even the appearance of unfairness. The quickest way for a corporation to lose a legal case is to let the opposing lawyer convince a jury that the corporation was unfair to someone. The same factor affects corporate morale the identical way.)

At its worst, this kind of thinking causes managers to think they are 'above the law'. At its best, this kind of thinking is corrosive to teamwork in any organization. Leaders would be seen doing the same things they told their followers to do. Another form of this is found in the old adage "Never ask someone to do something you wouldn't do".

One more thing. If the corporate rules are that employees fly coach class, than the CEO ought to fly coach also. Now you can also have another rule that says employees can pay out of their own pocket for the difference between coach fare and some other class of fare.

If the CEO wants to fly first class, and is making 100 to 1000 times the salary of many of his or her employees, the CEO can damn well afford to pay the difference themselves. The rules are the rules for everyone.

E. Being business-like does not mean you have to be mean and nasty.

Being business-like ought to mean making decisions based on the facts and logic of the business situation you are in. It does not mean that business decisions can be made with a callous disregard for the impact of those decisions on the personnel of the business.

A leader could not wash his or her hands of the consequences of a decision, simply because it was forced on them by external forces. Many managers I have seen over the years apparently believe that external pressure justifies them in being cold-hearted and callous when delivering bad news.

Yes, you have to do what you have to do. There are many ways to do things, generally, and you don't have to choose the path where your work and involvement in the resolution of the situation is minimized.

That's what it really amounts to. A leader needs to invest the extra time to help his subordinates deal with business decisions that adversely affect people. This doesn't mean that the leader needs to do everything personally. The leader needs to have taken the time and effort to provide as many coping mechanisms as possible given the situation he or she is facing.

Big corporations have HR departments that have resources that can help. Small businesses can turn to community organizations for help. The key point is that a leader will TRY.

F. Do Not be a Chiseler

Being frugal is not bad. However, there are limits.

In a local area in Pennsylvania, a township supervisor was quoted in the local newspaper as saying something to the effect that the reason taxes were so low was that the township was run on Pennsylvania Dutch principles, and the Pennsylvania Dutch were 'tightwads'. I don't think this gentleman realized that anywhere else in the country, he was not saying something complimentary about his constituents.

It used to be that supervisors and managers understood that you could not absolutely schedule most people's work day/week/month at a level of more than 80%. The remaining 20% would regularly be taken up with that portion of normal work occurrences like training, phone calls, unexpected unplanned work, trips to the supply cabinet, mental health breaks away from the desk, questions from colleagues, meetings and a hundred and one other things that inevitably occur in a work situation to reduce efficiency on 'the main task'.

Today, after a decade or more of being beaten up to better the bottom line and produce short term results at the cost of long term productivity, most managers have forgotten that you cannot have an infinitely elastic labor supply out of a fixed number of laborers. In short, you cannot continue to get more work out of people generally, and certainly without compensating them fairly for the increased level of work.

Most managers have no idea of what the 'real' workload is for their subordinates. There are actually scientific approaches, like job task analysis, that could be used to find out what a fair work load would be for a given job, but those take time, effort and money to accomplish.

So, managers give more and more work to people, and then wonder why turnover is high or morale is low. Managers refuse to determine what is low priority work and take the risk themselves of cancelling that work. So, their employees, faced with more work than anyone can do in a day, either take shortcuts that are not conducive to quality, or do their own submarining of work that they will never have time to accomplish.

These management behaviors might have worked with older generations of workers who thought they had an 'investment' in their workplaces and that companies would reward loyalty. All they are going to do for the new 'Millenials' and similar generations is increase the turnover rate, particularly in the gap between the Baby Boom generation and immediate following generations where the total numbers of available workers are going to be fewer than the total number of jobs that will be available.

Pardon me for another biblical reference: "Do not *bind the mouth* of the threshing *ox*." <Deut. 25.4>. In my Sunday School lessons, this was a allegory about equity. As the ox labored for its owner, it was entitled to support and there was an equity that it should be permitted to partake of the grain which it was threshing.

Give consideration always to the equity of the work situation you are calling for your subordinates to accomplish.

Another whole book could be written about wage equity in American business, and the compensation of executives.

Just remember that rewards deserve equity consideration also.

G. Say What You Mean and Mean What You Say

Nothing is more destructive to any human organization than to have its leaders not be believable by those they lead. You can have every Wall Street banker and analyst convinced that you are the next Warren Buffet, and if your employees think you are FOS, you are probably doomed right there. (For those of you not into texting, complete this phrase: Full Of _ _ _ _)

No, this doesn't mean that you have to tell everyone everything every time. What it does mean is that when you do say something, it should be accurate at the time and true. "I can't comment at this time" fits those attributes if used only when absolutely necessary.

The most common way in corporate America to violate these principles is to have a vision document that says you communicate in the organization "openly, honestly and using all ways", then allow managers to hoard information as a source of power.

In a leadership-based organization, the first time a leader found out that a subordinate was not passing along information, either Up or Down the chain, the leader would be out 'reaming a new one' at the earliest opportunity.

H. First try to convince people before you order them to do something

This is the biggest separating behavior between leaders and managers. Leaders know that if you convince a person, they will do what you want them to do, intelligently, for the right reasons, all the time.

Managers, stuck in the power trip of dominating people, don't see the need, or think they have the time, to do this leadership job.

Give the concept a fair trial. The next time a non-routine work item comes up that will be unpleasant for the person receiving it, do what you can to 'sell' the importance of the work to the company, to you, and how it might help fellow workers either do their jobs better, or see the example of how an 'excellent worker' deals with tough job experiences.

This is not something that is required for EVERY assignment or directive you hand out, but it is something that needs to be considered for non-routine and important new work items.

I.   Actually encourage people to present you with opposing points of view

This one actually takes courage and fortitude. (Admirable traits in many leaders).

You need to encourage your subordinates to communicate ANY reservations they have about your plans, orders, and any corporate strategy or direction. REALLY.

This needs to be done in ways that promote civility, honest discourse and open communication. All you have to be able to do is to CONSIDER FAIRLY the input, you do not have to ACCEPT it or AGREE with it. That is where most people go astray.

Most people take any UNINVITED criticism of their actions, plans, announcements or operations as PERSONAL criticism. That is one of the reasons that you need to invite the presentation to yourself of opposing views. If you have asked for it, it is less personal, and more detached, so you can handle it better personally.

Another reason is that you could have missed something, or be blinded by some factor that didn't allow you to consider some possibility. Hearing every argument against what you want to do, and defending against those arguments, and developing counters, actually does strengthen your case in the long run, as painful as it may seem to some to do this.

Sun Tzu, Chinese general and military strategist, urged future leaders to "Keep your friends close and your enemies closer", to be able to understand 'your enemy' better, this is another facet of this same strategy – learn all you can from the opposition of others.

Perhaps if British General Montgomery had been more receptive to Dutch Resistance warnings of increasing German strength in the area of Arnem, he might have had plans to deal with the possibility that the British 1st Airborne Division would have to deal with two under strength, but still formidable Panzer divisions when they dropped near "A Bridge Too Far". The results of this conceptual error was the destruction of that forlorn group as a fighting force.

As difficult as it will be, you also need to publicly praise people who bring you honest criticism, in meetings, memos or in private. Even when you disagree with the criticism or its basis.

This is not telling you to take abuse. Just advice, good or bad, that you need to consider. Advice that you have called for.

Too many CEO's build barriers to upward communication into the organization, and foster a corporate culture where asking for help from those above you is considered as not being a strong 'leader'. A real leader would make himself or herself available, and be concerned for the problems and challenges faced by the organization below them.

J.   Praise in public, discipline in private

This basic principle used to be taught specifically in classes on supervision. Somehow, in today's culture, it is a principle that seems to have been lost.

There are too many people, both managers and subordinates, who feel compelled to admonish other people in meetings and other public venues, primarily to show their power.

The advent of 'cubics' (work areas too small to even rate the term cubicle) for workstations and the habit of managers and supervisors of not calling people into their offices (or at least a conference room if they too don't have an office) for critical observations also shows a lack of understanding of this principle.

There are rare times when public floggings are necessary. A leader knows to minimize those and to effectively discipline his followers without humiliating or alienating them.

K. Communicate the Big Picture

Having vision is as useful as having a hallucination unless you can communicate that vision to others, and get them committed to follow it. If you can make people want to be part of your vision, and they can see how their participation will make a contribution to the final result, they will help you achieve that vision.

The first, and most important part, is communicating the scope and nature of where you want to go. As Dr. Steven Covey says in his story about organizing machete-wielders in the jungle, the leader climbs the tree and starts shouting "You're going the wrong way". That may work for a moment, but you also have to convey WHY they are going the wrong way, and what the right way is.

Ask yourself what convinced you that your vision was correct, and try to convey those elements to the people you want to work with you. Don't keep them in the dark and feed them... (a final mushroom reference)

L. Foster an Environment Where Everyone Feels Important on Some Level

People who are appreciated work better and harder. It doesn't require a degree in Psychology or Psychiatry to understand that. Your words and actions have the power to make people feel important to the success of an organization. Make it happen.

This is not about telling people something just to make them feel good, or not disciplining poor performers. It is about recognizing everyone has a contribution to make.

M. Communicate "What's In It For Them"

Telling people what a vision will do for the company is all well and good, but in today's climate, where it is obvious that corporations have no loyalty to their employees, it's not much of a motivator.

You also need to tailor something in your communications to catch the self-interest of each person. Some may want a challenging project to show 'how good they are'. Some may want power (careful now) and will want to be told how their work on a successful project will bring them recognition and greater opportunities. Team-oriented individuals will want to hear how they will be a part of a great team.

N. Be Positive About the Negative

Being honest about a bad situation is necessary, but it can get you into trouble if all you do is try to scare people into helping you. It might scare them into leaving, for example.

A leader needs to focus on his vision for solution of the problem and communicate that positive viewpoint. If things go wrong with the plan, have a contingency plan, and start thinking about a contingency plan for the contingency plan.

O. Put YOUR Money Where Your MOUTH Is

Nothing demonstrates to your people that you believe in what you are doing than putting something you value on the line.

It may be your prestige, it might be selling your corporate jet, or, as when Chrysler was in its first bankruptcy, it might be like Lee Iacocca cutting his salary to $1 a year until things got better.

A telling commentary on leadership in American business is the lack of such strong belief demonstrations during the economic crisis of 2008-2009. You had more CEO's defending bonuses to 'keep key employees' by a large margin than you had CEO's taking any action to show, without public pressure, that they accepted any responsibility for being in the crisis in the first place, or that felt they had to make such gestures in support of their companies.

P. If You Can't Lead, Manage to Lead
Ok, so you are not a great leader. You are a good manager though. What's the problem? It doesn't have to be your job to provide leadership.

Leadership doesn't always HAVE to come from the top. You can hire leaders and have them work for you. You can engage consultants to provide you with leadership expertise.

You can organize things according to the principles above so that you look and act like a leader. In 90% or more of life's situations, even this 'faking' it will be more than enough to stand out from today's crowd.

Maybe even, practicing the principles often enough will make you a leader in spite of yourself.

> *"Good leadership involves responsibility to the welfare of the group, which means that some people will get angry at your actions and decisions. It's inevitable, if you're honorable. Trying to get everyone to like you is a sign of mediocrity: you'll avoid the tough decisions, you'll avoid confronting the people who need to be confronted, and you'll avoid offering differential rewards based on differential performance because some people might get upset. Ironically, by procrastinating on the difficult choices, by trying not to get anyone mad, and by treating everyone equally "nicely" regardless of their contributions, you'll simply ensure that the only people you'll wind up angering are the most creative and productive people in the organization." General Colin Powell – A Leadership Primer*

Boat Race

The American and the British corporate offices for a large multi-national corporation decided to engage in a competitive boat race. Both teams practiced hard and long to reach their peak performance. On the big day they felt ready. The British won by a mile. Afterward, the American team was discouraged by the loss. Morale sagged. Corporate management decided that the reason for the crushing defeat had to be found, so a consulting firm was hired to investigate the problem and recommended corrective action.

The consultant's finding: The British team had eight people rowing and one person steering; the American team had one person rowing and eight people steering. After a year of study and millions spent analyzing the problem, the consultant firm concluded that too many people were steering and not enough were rowing on the American team.

So as race day neared again the following year, the American team's management structure was completely reorganized. The new structure: four steering managers, three area steering managers and a new performance review system for the person rowing the boat to provide work incentive. The next year, the British won by two miles. Humiliated, the American corporation laid off the rower for poor performance and gave the managers a bonus for discovering the problem....jokefile.co.uk

"Every man for himself and let the devil take the hindmost" – Old Proverb

CHAPTER 11

Greed is NOT Good

Michael Douglas tells the stockholders of Teldar Paper in the movie "Wall Street":

> *"The point is, ladies and gentlemen, that greed, for the lack of a better word, is good. Greed is right. Greed works. Greed clarifies, cuts through, and captures, the essence of the evolutionary spirit. Greed in all of its forms, greed for life, for money, for love, for knowledge, has marked the upward surge of mankind."*

The one item of greed he left out of his list was the greed for power or control.

I contend that two various forms of greed have corrupted corporate America to the point where our ability to respond to structural changes in the business climate (e.g. world competition for commerce) have been compromised.

The first is greed for short-term profits, a.k.a the 'bottom line' at the expense of long-term viability. Listen in on any earnings conference call or webcast for a Fortune 500 company and you are most likely to hear all about this quarter's earnings, or the earnings per share for the rest of the year. What do you hear about the future of the company?

At best, what you will find is a projection of earnings per share for the next few years. Now of course, you are going to say, 'what would you expect in an earnings or financial conference call?'" That's missing the point.

The point is, the focus is precisely on earnings, and only earnings, with predominance given to the earnings right now. Where are the corporate conference calls on the future of the industry they are in and what actions the CEO sees necessary to position the company for growth into the future? Where are the statements that dividend growth should be halted so that large investments in company infrastructure to prepare for the future should be made?

Yes, I know investors bear part of the responsibility for driving this with their seemingly insatiable desire to have their stock prices and dividends only go up, and at unsustainable levels. (Why do you think Ponzi schemes continue to work nearly one hundred years after the scam was introduced to the United States? Bernie Madoff promised steady returns produced both in up and down markets and his scheme persisted for decades before it fell apart.)

The problem is that corporate officers have failed to show much leadership or backbone to try and stop this nonsense. Instead they have engaged in all kinds of financial manipulations to try and make investors 'happy'.

If more leadership skills were applied, maybe they could convince their shareholders that they were taking their companies in the right directions that would produce value in the future, and increase the long-term viability of the company. In 2009 as I write this, I see companies like Ford, GM and Chrysler having their stock devalued to ridiculous levels, and some going into bankruptcy, mainly due to lack of leadership to make the hard choices that were needed several years ago. It was easy to postpone decisions when things were on a roll that made it easy to keep playing the game of perpetual greed.

The second greed comes from the lust for power. Increasingly, it seems, the motivation for our top corporate managers is not the amount they accomplish for bettering the corporation, or anyone else besides themselves. The motivation factor is now how much power they can accumulate for themselves over other people.

My observation is that a leader who has real power doesn't need to flaunt it.

So, tell me what the real purpose is for so many executive perks provided to today's management? Start with chauffeured Lincolns, Cadillacs or Mercedes. The argument here is usually that the executive can be more effective if he or she can 'work' from the backseat while they drive in to work. Maybe if they have a 1 or two hour commute in a major city perhaps, but many have 15 or 20 minute commutes also. Remember this 'productivity' argument is what is used to justify using a cell phone while driving too.

The natural extension is to corporate jets. Then we find out that some contracts make the jets available to the executives wives to go on shopping trips. My contention is that these perks are just more ways to show how much 'power' these people have. How transitory that kind of 'power' is was demonstrated in 2009 when auto manufacturers CEO's made their first trip to Washington, DC, to ask for bailout money in their corporate jets. The public furor had them driving back the next time in hybrids. Leaders would have known better. Managers couldn't see what the big problem was.

These 'power trips' have been going on for millennia, I know. It is just sad to see how many people have failed to learn the lessons of history, and are therefore condemning us to see them repeated in business time after time.

The last thing I want to comment on is the trend toward lack of real social responsibility in corporations. This is another sign of the lack of leadership fundamentals in American business operations.

Now before the fundamentalist conservatives (with the big C) start frothing at the mouth, this isn't about welfare or global warming or even the glass ceiling. My contention is that not only have corporations removed employer-employee loyalty considerations, they have also tainted their ethical responsibilities as members of a community.

Strong words, but not as strong as you might be thinking, because I use the classical definition of ethics "Duty owed to a group because of membership in that group." Most often today, ethics, morality and legality are often confused, primarily by mis-named 'ethics laws'.

Quite simply, you have the phrase 'good corporate citizen' thrown around a lot, primarily talking about corporations that make a lot of donations to charities and get a lot of good press about their 'involvement' with the community.

While some of this is undoubtedly done out of real personal commitment, particularly by the CEO of a company, a whole lot more of it is being done in the cause of shameless self-promotion. The causes are being selected not by their charitable appeal to the employees of the company, but by their promotional benefit to the company. Understand, then, that this is not knocking any particular charity. The problem is the way leaderless companies go about using charitable contributions for their own self-serving purposes.

A company is a legal 'fictitious person'. Any person who is a member of the community has an ethical duty to the rest of the community. What that duty is, will be decided by the community, not the person. In America, most persons believe that charity is a personal choice, and it should be a private matter.

Managers want efficiency and they want to receive something for their efforts. So what do we get today? Something I will call the "General Approach" so as not to pick on any specific charitable agency.

From on-high, the word goes out, "We will have a General Approach campaign". Someone in the management chain, high enough to look somewhat important, but not a VP, or viewed as having too much 'real work' to do, is 'volunteered' as the campaign chairman. A manager pushed to the side to do "special projects' is a frequent choice.

Then all the supervisors and managers of the company are told to find 'volunteer' canvassers, whose job it is to go to each and every employee in their group and solicit 'pledges', to be taken out of their paycheck by payroll deduction. I'm told that some people actually do ask for this assignment, but in the organizations I've been in, people more often try to find ways to get out of town or become inconspicuous when the search is on for these 'volunteers'.

Then, to complete the picture, statistics are kept and published around the organization, not just of how much money has been collected for the campaign, but of things like what percentage of the employees of each department or group have 'participated', using various measures like returned pledge cards, number of payroll deductions, or other indicators.

Some really crass managers even try to liven up the 'competition' by offering to do things like bring in donuts once a week for a month if their groups' numbers beat some other group. The emphasis is on meeting corporate goals for the campaign. If their group is not "100%", I've seen canvassers get heat to disclose who hasn't returned a pledge card, even if that information is supposed to be 'confidential'. Of course now, the payroll department has to know who has returned a pledge card so their paycheck can be docked.

The best ways in which you can judge whether or not all of this effort is for pure charity or corporate image-building, are two-fold: First see who goes to the annual charity awards banquet, with the requisite PR photographers, and second, see how often the charity is mentioned the rest of the year, when the campaign is not in gear, particularly by the CEO.

If the campaign manager and the canvasser who got the most money for the charity go to the banquet and accept the awards, your company is a more likely a genuine citizen of your community. If the CEO is shown accepting the award in the company newsletter, and the same photo happens to appear in the local papers, you might have some motivation concerns.

My basic point is, that if companies and CEO's were such good citizens, the contributions would come from their profits, and not from trying to browbeat them from their employees, especially under circumstances that lower their employees privacy on their charitable giving. A caring leader might try to convince employees to give, but it wouldn't be implemented the way it is now. There also wouldn't be so much emphasis on the publicity value. The current 'charitable' system reeks of being well-managed.

> *"...reckless greed and risk taking...must never endanger*
> *our prosperity again"*
> *–President-elect Barack Obama*

Why you and the boss are totally different

When you take a long time, you're slow.
When your boss takes a long time, he's thorough.

When you don't do it, you're lazy.
When your boss doesn't do it, he's too busy.

When you make a mistake, you're an idiot.
When your boss makes a mistake, he's only human.

When doing something without being told, you're overstepping your authority.
When your boss does the same thing, that's initiative.

When you take a stand, you're being bull-headed.
When your boss does it, he's being firm.

When you overlooked a rule of etiquette, you're being rude.
When your boss skips a few rules, he's being original.

When you please your boss, you're apple polishing.
When your boss pleases his boss, he's being co-operative.

When you're out of the office, you're wandering around.
When your boss is out of the office, he's on business.

When you're on a day off sick, you're always sick.
When your boss is a day off sick, he must be very ill.

When you apply for leave, you must be going for an interview.
When your boss applies for leave, it's because he's overworked.

Jokefile.co.uk

"You ask, what is our aim? I can answer in one word. It is victory! Victory at all costs! Victory in spite of all terrors. Victory, however long and hard the road may be, for without victory, there is no survival." –Winston Churchill

CHAPTER 12

The Bottom Line?

A leader cares about the followers he has. A leader cares about his organization, the people in it, and the goals he wants to lead those people to. A leader treats people as people.

A manager treats everything as 'resources', including people. A manager generally cares most about his work getting done. There is a big difference in these two outlooks.

Leadership is not just 'managing' people efficiently. Just because you are at the top of the management chain does not make you able to claim you are 'part of the leadership team'. You definitely are part of the management team, but if that management shows no leadership properties, you should not be calling yourself a leader.

You can't appoint anyone, including yourself a leader. Leaders are elected by the followers that you have convinced, energized, prepared and nurtured to have a common vision and goals to better your organization and its mission. Winning that election makes you a leader. Not even holding the election makes you a manager.

There is a difference between the engagement a worker has in investing themselves in outstanding job performance, and the commitment a worker has to their employer. A manager would be happy with the former alone, while a leader would strive for both together.

Professor Thomas Brit, of Clemson University summarizes why this difference will eventually make a difference to American business:

> *"When the economy is experiencing a general downturn, it may be unlikely that engaged employees low in organizational commitment can find another position. But if they do have the opportunity to change jobs they will.*
>
> *Managers who fail to position employees to be effective in their roles and provide organizational support may lose their most talented and energetic people.*
>
> *The ones who stay behind may well be the ones who just don't care, "*

In a global economy, where people can now work for companies in any country, sometimes without even leaving their homes or home countries, we can't keep pushing the best and brightest out of our companies because we can't do anything but manage them.

American business needs more leaders, <u>now</u>. We have plenty of managers to go around already. We don't need more managers creating organizations with legions of workers who don't care anymore. We need to stop managers from trying to suck employees out of their equations.

Prepare yourself, prepare others, be a leader. Help put American business back on the road to recovery.

> *"If you are a real coach, a real leader, preparation (of players) is the thing, that's what you do."*
> *–Bo Schembechler*

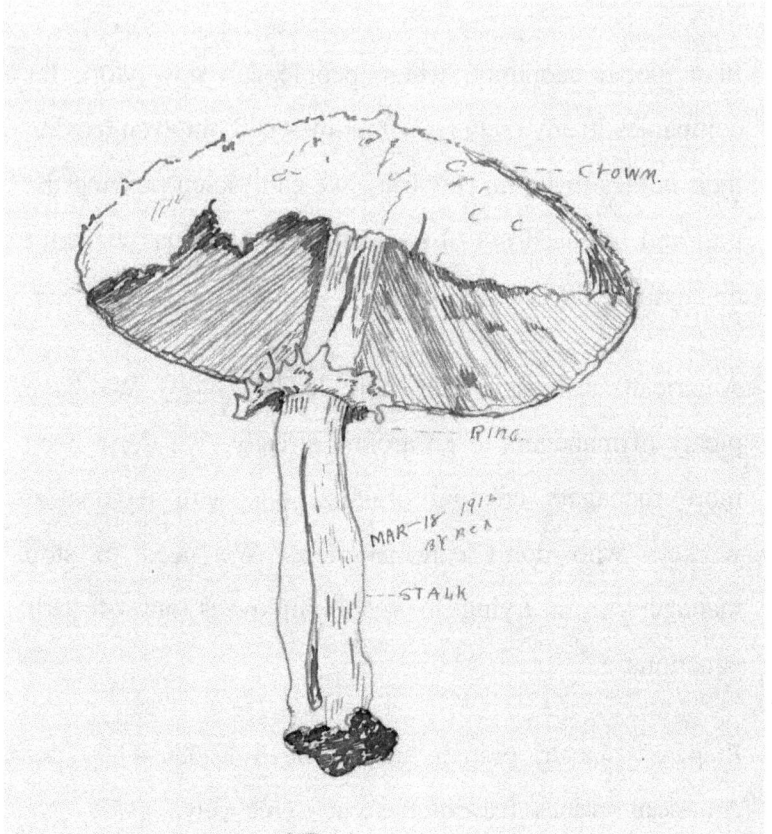

Labels on sketch: CROWN, RING, MAR-18 1916 BY REX, STALK

*This pen and ink sketch of a mushroom is from the
1916 Dugger (Indiana) High School biology notebook
of Rexford Ballard. Rex died from the effects of wounds
suffered during WWI. The Rexford Ballard American
Legion Post 224 is named in his honor. He died so that
we could have the freedom to argue things like the
merits of leadership over managership.*

www.ingramcontent.com/pod-product-compliance
Lightning Source LLC
Chambersburg PA
CBHW060041210326
41520CB00009B/1216